HOW DOES YOUR GARDEN GROW?

OTHER GARDENING BOOKS PUBLISHED BY CROOM HELM

Growing Fuchsias
K. Jennings and V. Miller

Growing Hardy Perennials
Kenneth A. Beckett

Growing Dahlias
Philip Damp

Growing Irises
G. E. Cassidy and S. Linnegar

Growing Cyclamen
Gay Nightingale

Violets
Roy E. Coombs

Plant Hunting in Nepal
Roy Lancaster

Slipper Orchids
Robin Graham with
Ronald Roy

Growing Chrysanthemums
Harry Randall and Alan Wren

Waterlilies
Philip Swindells

Climbing Plants
Kenneth A. Beckett

1000 Decorative Plants
J.L. Krempin

Better Gardening
Robin Lane Fox

Country Enterprise
Jonathan and Heather Ffrench

*The Rock Gardener's
Handbook*
Alan Titchmarsh

Growing Bulbs
Martyn Rix

Victorians and their Flowers
Nicolette Scourse

Growing Begonias
E. Catterall

Growing Roses
Michael Gibson

*The Water Gardener's
Handbook*
Philip Swindells

The Salad Garden
Elisabeth Arter

The Pelargonium Family
William J. Webb

Hardy Geraniums
Peter F. Yeo

*The Handbook of Soft
Fruit Growing*
Ken Muir and David Turner

Growing Lilies
Derek Fox

HOW DOES YOUR GARDEN GROW?

Peter Hillman

CROOM HELM

London · Sydney · Dover, New Hampshire

© 1985 Peter Hillman
Croom Helm Ltd, Provident House, Burrell Row
Beckenham, Kent BR3 1AT
Croom Helm Australia Pty Ltd, Suite 4, 6th Floor,
64-76 Kippax Street, Surry Hills, NSW 2010, Australia

British Library Cataloguing in Publication Data

Hillman, Peter
  How does your garden grow?: simple garden
  science
  1. Gardening
  I. Title
  635   SB450.97

ISBN 0-7099-3711-3

Croom Helm, 51 Washington Street,
Dover, New Hampshire, 03820, USA

Library of Congress Cataloging in Publication Data

Hillman, Peter
  How does your garden grow?
  Includes index.
  1. Gardening.   2. Botany.   I. Title.
SB453.H656   1985   635   85-16653

ISBN 0-7099-3711-3 (U.S.)

Typeset by Columns of Reading
Printed and bound in Great Britain by
Biddles Ltd, Guildford and King's Lynn

CONTENTS

List of Figures   vii
List of Tables   viii

1 Introduction   1
Gilbert White – the First Great
British Naturalist   1
How Plant Names Work   3
What Does 'Hardiness'
Mean?   6

2 When is a Flower Not a Flower?   10
Flowering Plants – the
Angiosperms   10
How It All Began   12
Conifers – the Gymno-
sperms   14
Ferns   18
Mosses   20

3 Flower Power   22
Classification   22
Families of Flowers   26
The Genetics of
Pollination   30
Pollination   32
Mendel's Theory of
Inheritance   34
Breeding Your Own
Plants   37
Seed Success   38
Seed Sowing   40
Selecting a Seedling   41

4 Plumbing Problems   43
Leaf Structure and
Function   43
Photosynthesis   45
Transpiration   48
Stems – the Support
System   49
Roots – the Anchorage
System   50
Hormones   52
Flowering Time   54
Bark   55

5 Can You Dig It?   57
Soil Structure and
Texture   57
Soil is a Living Thing   60
Improving Your Soil   62
What Does 'pH' Mean?   64
Composts and Mixes   66
The Great Debate – Soil or
Peat-based Mixtures?   68

6 Where There's Muck There's Magic   69
Humus   69
FYM   69
Composing a Compost   70
Aerobic Composting   71
Anaerobic Composting   73
Mulches   74
Peat   75

7 Food, Glorious Food   79
A Healthy Diet   79
'The Big Three' – Nitrogen,
Phosphates and Potash   79
Two Important Allies –
Calcium and Magnesium   81
The Trace Elements   83
Organic Versus Inorganic
Fertilisers   83
Types of Fertilisers   84
Too Much or Too Little
Food   87
Carnivorous Plants   88

8 Protect and Survive 91
Growing Under Glass 91
Heating Your Green-
house 96
The History of Green-
houses 97

9 The Secret of
Immortality? 101
Mary Ann's Apple 101
Offsets and Plantlets 101
Propagation by Cuttings 102
Propagation by Grafting 104
Cell Manipulation 107

10 Are All Gardeners
Trouble-makers? 110
Asking for Trouble 110
Categories of Pesticides 110
How Safe Are Garden
Chemicals? 111
Types of Pesticide 116
Play It Safe 117

Aphids 118
Friends of the Gardener 118
Viruses 119

11 I Hoe, I Hoe . . . 122
To Hoe or Not to Hoe 122
Single Digging, Double
Digging and No-digging 123
Regular Rotation 124
Pruning 126
Weeds – the Gardeners'
Common Enemy 127

12 The Shape of Things
to Come? 132
Short-term Prospects 132
Natural Improvements 133
Product Progress 135
Long-term Prospects 136
Conclusions 137

Index 138

Figures

1.1 Approximate Boundaries of Zones of Hardiness   8
2.1 Flower Structure   10
2.2 The Life Cycle of Conifers   15
2.3 The Life of a Fern   19
2.4 The Life of a Moss   21
3.1 Monocots and Dicots   23
3.2 The Flower Life Story   24
3.3 *Rosaceae* Flower Structure   27
3.4 *Papilionaceae* Flower Structure   28
3.5 *Orchidaceae* Flower Structure   28
3.6 The Flower Structure of Grasses   29
3.7 Broad Bean Chromosomes   31
3.8 Mendel's Pea Breading Experiment   34
4.1 The Leaf Story   44
4.2 The Leaf Revealed   45
4.3 Photosynthesis   46
4.4 The Stem Story   50
4.5 What Happens When Plants Go Woody   55
5.1 Sand, Silt and Clay Particles   57
5.2 The Hillman Handful Soil Test   59
5.3 Flocculation of Clay in Soils   64
5.4 Do It Yourself Soil pH Test   65
6.1 An Aerobic Compost Heap   72
7.1 The Availability of Plant Foods and Numbers of Living Things in Soils of Different pH   87
8.1 Why a Greenhouse Heats Up   92
8.2 Greenhouses   95
8.3 A Miniature Rain Forest   99
9.1 Ten Years' Growth of Different Rootstocks   105
9.2 Graft Your Own Tree   106
9.3 How to Clone an Orchid   109
10.1 Learn Your Labels   114
11.1 Double Digging   123
11.2 A Three-year Vegetable Plot Rotation   125
12.1 A Multicrop Plant   133

Tables

1.1 Some Latin 'A's'   7
7.1 Fertiliser Ingredients and Their Uses   80
7.2 Amounts of Hydrated Lime Needed to Raise the pH Level to 6.5   82
7.3 Understanding the Organics   85
7.4 Understanding the Inorganics   86
8.1 Pick-a-position then Pick-a-plant   94
9.1 How Tall Do You Want Your Fruit Trees?   105
10.1 Which Pesticide?   112
10.2 Which Fungicide?   113
10.3 Golden Rules for Using Pesticides   120
11.1 Which Herbicide?   128

Dedicated to
my grandfather, Jack, a gardener of the
last generation,
my mother and father and Chris and
Terry, gardeners of today's generation,
and Sarah and Emma, the gardeners of the
next generation.

1 Introduction

GILBERT WHITE – THE FIRST GREAT BRITISH NATURALIST

This book is designed to introduce the beginner to the fundamentals of gardening and the more experienced amateur to the scientific theory behind the practical work. It will be a simple, often lighthearted, but informative stroll through the horticultural principles which are often clouded by technical jargon.

The idea that any interested person can look into the scientific reasons behind nature is, of course, not new. In 1720, when the apple-watching genius Isaac Newton was still alive, a man called Gilbert White was born at Selborne in Hampshire. He was destined to become the first great British naturalist. Apart from his description of birds and bats, other animals and plants were investigated. His discovery and naming of the harvest-mouse, the inquiry into the bacterial attack on a vine which he called a 'filthy annoyance' and his experimentation into worm activities have now become legendary. Who else would think to go out onto their lawn on a winter's night, in order to watch earthworms mate?

He recorded an emigration of blackflies in 1785. People, as well as hedges and vegetables, were coated by these black aphids. White's onion beds were coated with the pest for six days. He concluded that these animals had come from the Kent hop fields because of the prevailing winds at the time.

Even folklore was put into writing by White, although he believed it to be superstitious rubbish. He recorded that young ash trees were split lengthways, wedged open and 'ruptured children' were stripped naked and pushed through the apertures to cure them. If the two halves of the sapling recovered and the tree grew properly the child was thought to be cured.

Other trees were considered by White purely for their beauty. Beech was thought to be the most lovely of all the forest trees because of its smooth bark, shiny leaves and graceful branching.

The natural history that White put down in *The Natural History of Selborne* became immortal but you too can add a new, valuable, dimension to your enjoyment of gardening.

For example, have you ever stopped to think about why some plants that you care for fail to grow and others thrive? This can only be understood when you know what makes flowering plants different from ferns and other types of plants. We will investigate this topic later along with various types of garden tool, soil make-up, compost and fertilisers.

We will rediscover the 'Hells Angel' of the garden world, otherwise called the aphid, that White loved to hate. We will travel, in our imagination, with the lowly earthworm and see what a valuable animal it really is. Plant diseases will be explained too because only when we understand how a disease works can effective action be taken to prevent it or attack it if it does strike our favourite geranium or orchid.

The folklore of so-called 'green fingers' and talking to plants will be dealt with because even these tales repay closer examination. We do not use split ash trees any longer, although it might be a final resort to cure the effects of a hard day's digging!

Over the past few seasons the seed catalogues have listed expensive F_1 hybrids. What these are, why they are expensive, how to produce your own F_1, and for that matter F_2 hybrids too, will be explained.

Other famous personalities will appear later in the text but the most famous must be Charles Darwin. As we will see he had a part to play in the explanation of plant breeding as well as the theory of evolution so often associated with his name.

The name of Stephen Hales, a neighbour of Gilbert White, will appear too. He was one of the first people to try and explain the uptake of water by plants. Using modern knowledge we can look inside the plant's stem, root and leaf to see what is going on and why water is so essential.

For more fortunate, and adventurous, gardeners the use of greenhouses and other protective structures has meant that plants normally unheard of in gardens can be cultivated with ease. However, only by understanding just how the greenhouse environment is different from that outside can the best results be obtained.

The modern-day ability to produce many identical plants from a single parent is very exciting but nothing new to the world of gardening. Taking cuttings and other forms of propagation have been common practice for many years but micropropagation is a new and even more exciting option now available to horticulturalists. The theory behind these practices will be explained.

The growth of any living thing, be it plant or animal, is a wondrous process. In plants as well as animals, it is controlled by chemicals called hormones. Gardeners use these to modify plant growth, to make plants root, to dwarf *Chrysanthemums*, and so on. How they work and are used will be elucidated along with many other common gardening techniques.

What the long-term future holds for the gardener can only be guessed at but in the short term, within the next five years, some clear trends can be seen. We will look into this 'window of the future' and see what it holds for us.

Before we begin this voyage into horticulture three questions need to be answered. First, why is Latin used for plant names? Secondly, what is meant by the terms species, varieties and cultivars? Thirdly, what do gardeners mean by hardiness?

HOW PLANT NAMES WORK

Some gardeners maintain that Latin is used in naming living things purely to make their study exclusive – nothing is further from the truth. The important point is that a common language is used so that any gardener, be they British, North American, Chinese, or from any nation, can use it and converse meaningfully with gardeners from other nations. Everyone knows what

Asparagus plumosus looks like but comparatively few call it the Asparagus fern. Equally, few know the common name of montbretia but no one can mistake *Tritonia × crocosmilflora*. How many could recognise the Pride of India or China tree by common name but everyone could identify *Koelreuteria paniculata* without ambiguity.

Who was responsible for this? Another contemporary of Gilbert White – the Swedish botanist Carl Linnaeus – who tried to make sense of the vast numbers of living creatures and plants known at the time. Since Latin was then the international language of science and scholarship, rather like English is today, it was the obvious choice for his system.

He began with plant **families**. Rather like our own families these consist of many members or sometimes just one. The *Rosaceae* family contains all the roses and their relatives, *Orchidaceae* the orchids, *Papilionaceae* the pea family, and so on. All members of a family will share common characteristics like flower structure or arrangement of leaves.

Further down the scale comes the **genus**. The plants in each genus are related to each other rather like distant cousins are related. Maples are in the *Acer* genus, daisies in the *Bellis* genus and ivies in the *Hedera* genus.

Whereas the genus name is the equivalent of a surname, and always has a capital letter, the **species** name is like a Christian name. So the species *vulgaris* means 'common' and heather becomes *Calluna vulgaris*. Ivy becomes *Hedera helix*, an ivy which twines, and so on.

Since the days of Linnaeus mankind has discovered that there are over 230,000 species of flowering plants. We also know that there are over 700 species of conifers and 10,000 species of fern. Thankfully, the same system can be used to place correctly all of these.

Now for varieties, cultivars and hybrids. **Varieties** are plants of a species which have distant characters that make them different from all the other plants of that species. They occur naturally like the so-called coffin juniper which, like other varieties, is named by its genus, then species, then variety (var.) and so is more properly called *Juniperus recurva* var. *coxii*. This variety is taller, thinner and has brighter green drooping shoots than the species. Notice that all Latin names are normally given in italics.

Cultivars are 'man-made' varieties, that is they arise during cultivation. Their names are always given in ordinary type but in single quotation marks. Take the tulips for example. They all belong to the genus *Tulipa* and there are many species but the total number of cultivars is mind-boggling. One could easily obtain 150 cultivars, each of which would show different plant shape and size, form, colour and flowering times. They would range from the cultivar called 'Brilliant Star' – a scarlet flower which appears in April – to the much taller cultivar called 'La Tulipe Noire' which despite its name is a dark purple and not black.

Hybrids are the result of breeding between two genera (the plural of genus) or species (here the plural is the same as the singular). Normally hybrids can be distinguished by the sign '×'. For example, *Aesculus* × *carnea* (the red horse chestnut) is a hybrid species between *A. hippocastanum* (the common horse chestnut) and *A. pavia* (the red buckeye). Similarly × *Fatshedera* is a hybrid genus, the foliage plant × *F. lizei* is a common houseplant which is a result of a cross between *Hedera hibernica* (the Irish ivy) and *Fatsia japonica*.

Sometimes more than two genera are involved, this is common for the orchids. Names like × *Brassolaeliocattleya* show that the three orchid genera *Brassavola*, *Laelia* and *Cattleya* are involved.

Horticulturalists have a habit of changing their mind and so new names, especially for genera and species often appear. That very fine tree, the noble fir, with its blue-grey needles and upward pointing brown cones, has changed its species name from *nobilis* to *procera* but so that the 'old hands' can still recognise it, it is always listed with its alternative name or synonym (abbreviated as syn.) as *Abies procera* syn. *Abies nobilis*.

Lastly, in spite of all these efforts to simplify the naming of our garden plants some varieties have, in the past, picked up very unwieldly names. Try *Chamaecyparis pisifera* 'Plumosa Aurea Nana'. Although this little gem of a golden conifer deserves a fitting title, it is all a bit much when you consider that it is only 3 ft (90 cm) tall and 2 ft (60 cm) across. One wonders what name could be conjured up for the biggest tree in the world, the redwood of California, which reaches to almost 370 ft (110 m) tall. It comes as a disappointment to know that it is labelled as *Sequoia sempervirens*. So plant names are no indication of plant size.

Interestingly, this redwood is said to have been introduced to the gardening world by a down-and-out gold miner from New York who, while prospecting in California in the 1850s, was showered by seeds from the tree as a consequence of squirrels feeding on the cones above. A stroke of inspiration made him fill his snuff box with the seeds and sell them to a New York nursery. Soon everyone who was anyone in America and Europe wanted an avenue lined with redwood trees.

Once the Latin names are decided upon, what do they mean? Well, translation is not always a clear-cut and painless process so the English equivalent of a Latin word tends to be more like a sentence than a single word. Take the genus *Begonia* for example, this great group of ornamental plants is named after a Governor of French Canada by the name of Michael Begon (1636-1710). He was a great patron of botany and so in return for sponsoring plant-hunting expeditions he had the compliment of many plants being named after him.

Apart from being named after people plants can be named after their properties. For example, the word *tectorum* as in *Sempervivum tectorum*, otherwise known as the common houseleek, signifies they have something to do with roofs. The houseleek grows freely on stone and slate roofs so its Latin name comes as no surprise. Indeed it is thought by some folk that this plant gives protection against lightning and so it has been deliberately planted on roofs. Whether the houseleeks really work as a lightning conductor is not known but many roofs have been coated with houseleeks as a result.

So Latin names have meanings which sometimes have historical references and often indicate special features about that plant.

WHAT DOES HARDINESS MEAN?

Every plant catalogue of every nation refers to the hardiness of its specimens yet the term hardy is rather vague. Overall, what you can be certain of is that a plant said to be hardy in a given area will grow there all the year round without protection. Obviously the climate of any area is created by a combination of factors including: latitude (how far north or south of the equator a place is), altitude (how far above sea level an area is), aspect (what direction a garden faces) and exposure (whether it is sheltered or not).

The presence of a large lake or sea or ocean near to a garden will ensure that winter temperatures are not so low as they would be otherwise. Water warms up and cools down slowly so during cold periods it will release its heat. However, salt-laden winds are injurious to plants so it is not all good news for seaside gardeners.

Even within a given area the garden can provide local conditions which make possible the growth of otherwise

Table 1.1 Some Latin 'A's'

Latin names	Translation
a-	Prefix meaning 'lacking', e.g. *apetalus* means lacking petals.
Abies	Fir.
-aceae	Word ending meaning 'belonging to', e.g. *Rosaceae* – belonging to the rose family.
Abutilon	Flowering Maple.
Acanthus	Thorn or prickle.
Acer	Sharp. Romans used maple for spear hafts.
Achillea	Yarrow.
Acorus	Sweet Flag.
Adiantum	Dry. Maidenhair fern fronds will remain dry when plunged into water.
Agave	Admirable, e.g. flowers of sisal plant.
Agrostis	A kind of grass.
alb-, albi-, albo-	Prefix meaning white, e.g. *albidus*.
Allium	Garlic and related plants, e.g. onions.
alpinus	Alpine, strictly speaking the plants from the high mountains above the tree line.
amabilis	Lovely.
americanus	From North or South America.
anglicus	From England.
annuus	Annual plant.
Aquilegia	An eagle, from the form of the flowers in columbine.
argentea	Silvery.
Aspidistra	Small round shield, from shape of female part of flower.
atro-	Prefix meaning dark, e.g. *atropurpureus* – dark purple.
aureus	Golden.
Azalea	Dry, referring to the original species found in dry places in Lapland.

tender plants, those that are harmed by low temperatures, or choice plants, those that need a particular kind of soil. For example, by planting grape vines (*Vitis* species) next to south-facing walls more of the sun's heat is obtained and there is less chance of frost damage.

Also, by providing very acidic compost *Rhododendrons*, including the azaleas, can be cultivated, even in an alkaline soil area like that created by limestone or chalk bedrock.

Anyway, although local conditions vary such a lot and even the same plant may differ in its hardiness as it ages or even between towns in the same region, it is still useful to have some guide as to where plants are generally thought to be hardy.

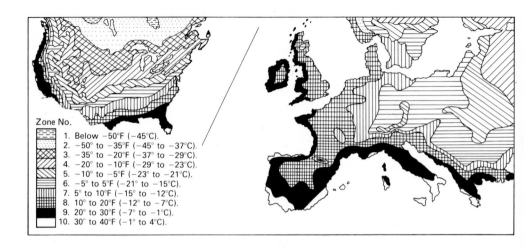

Zone No.
1. Below −50°F (−45°C).
2. −50° to −35°F (−45° to −37°C).
3. −35° to −20°F (−37° to −29°C).
4. −20° to −10°F (−29° to −23°C).
5. −10° to −5°F (−23° to −21°C).
6. −5° to 5°F (−21° to −15°C).
7. 5° to 10°F (−15° to −12°C).
8. 10° to 20°F (−12° to −7°C).
9. 20° to 30°F (−7° to −1°C).
10. 30° to 40°F (−1° to 4°C).

Figure 1.1 Approximate Boundaries of Zones of Hardiness

To give an example: because Seville oranges (*Citrus bigaradia*) are hardy in Zones 9 and 10 they may well be half-hardy – needing protection from frost – in Zone 8 and perhaps greenhouse cultivation is the answer here. Although by now you may wish to move to south Florida, it is best to remember that not all plants need to have the high temperatures experienced in Zone 10. Although this may suit citrus fruits (oranges, lemons, limes, mandarins, grapefruits and hybrid fruits) deciduous fruit trees, those that lose their leaves in winter unlike the evergreen citrus, require a dormant period every season and low winter temperatures enable this to occur. So for those who prefer apples, pears, plums as well as cane fruits, currants and gooseberries they would do better to live in northern or eastern USA or the British Isles or the greatest part of Europe.

The zones shown in Figure 1.1 are based on a system

first devised by the Arnold Arboretum of Harvard University in the United States of America. There are ten zones in all and each one has a particular range of lowest yearly temperature (in fact the average, annual minimum temperatures). Those plants which are found in Zone 1 normally experience temperatures as low as $-50°F$ ($-45°C$) whereas those of Zone 10 have lowest temperatures of only $30°$ to $40°F$ ($-1°$ to $+4°C$). If you locate the place where you live Figure 1.2 will give an immediate guide to the lowest temperatures likely to be experienced in that region. Because of the size of the USA and Canada all ten zones are to be found there whereas in the British Isles only three zones exist and one of these, Zone 6, is restricted to a part of eastern Scotland.

Lastly, the map of hardiness zones takes no account of rainfall or, as the meteorologists – weather forecasters – say, precipitation. Each plant has particular water requirements which usually vary throughout the growing season. Droughts will eventually lead to the death of plants, even cacti will eventually give up but this might take over ten years as opposed to some of the delicate ferns which will expire after only a few hours without sufficient water.

Waterlogging on the other hand is bad news for plants for many reasons. Rain wets the leaves and stems making them prone to fungal attack and flowers and fruit may not develop. After the soil feels the effects the roots may suffocate, die and rot.

The groundwork has now been laid for a proper expedition of the imagination into the world of gardening. This discovery of the secrets of horticulture is a fascinating journey which will begin with the plants that most people prize above all others – the flowering plants.

2 When is a Flower Not a Flower?

FLOWERING PLANTS – THE ANGIOSPERMS

Imagine a world without flowers. Imagine a seed catalogue without flowers. Impossible! The real flowers fill gardens, houses, offices and those parts that they cannot reach are occupied by plastic imitations and photographs. But what makes a flower a flower and not something else?

Obviously, all flowering plants possess a flower of some sort – but what is a flower? A flower is a reproductive organ, and a very successful one at that because of the sheer numbers of flowering plants in the world, nearly a quarter of a million species – and those are just the ones that have so far been found.

Another name for a flowering plant is Angiosperm which means 'enclosed seed'. This is because once the flower has performed its function the seed or seeds that have been made are enclosed within the ovary, a characteristic unique to Angiosperms (see Figure 2.1).

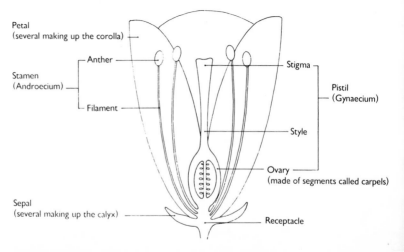

Figure 2.1 Flower Structure

The outermost part of the flower consists of protective leaves called sepals. These protect the flower when it is in bud and are usually green. There are notable exceptions, though, such as *Fuchsias* and, perhaps the most common example, the daffodils (*Narcissus* species) where the sepals are yellow.

Next come the petals. These are modified leaves, although to see a pansy, carnation or rose flower makes this difficult to believe. Their function is to attract pollinators – from large ones such as hummingbirds to small ones such as insects. One point to remember, though, is that insects see flowers in a different way. Although humans cannot see ultra-violet light the insects can. To flies and beetles the whites, pinks and reds of the foxgloves (*Digitalis* species) are of great fascination. It is the dark spots on the 'throat' of the flower that are of most interest to animal life. The contrasting dark and light areas indicate that food is available for the caller. A glance at most flowers will reveal the same patterns; pinks and carnations (*Dianthus* species) with their rings of contrasting colour, the dark lines on *Pelargonium* blooms and, perhaps the most spectacular of all, the orchids.

There are about 20,000 species of orchid and that takes no account of the hybrids. It is a very successful family which has members in every climate except the arid and ice deserts. The lines, dots and blotches to be found on orchid flowers defy full description but they range from the pure white petals and sepals and rose-purple striped lip of the slipper orchid, *Cypripedium reginae*, through to the vibrant chestnut brown and yellow tiger orchid, *Odontoglossum grande*. Incidentally, orchids only thrive when given lots of moisture, high day and cool night temperatures, protection from direct sunlight and good ventilation.

Returning to the flower structure, in the centre of the flower are the most essential, and best protected, parts. They consist of the male pollen-bearing stamens and female pistil. Broadly speaking, in order to obtain more flowering plants the pollen from the same or another plant of the same species has to be transferred to the uppermost part of the pistil. This transfer is called pollination and is so important that it will be dealt with later as a separate topic.

What else do flowering plants have apart from flowers, though? They also have well-developed leaves, roots and stems.

Leaves are the 'factories' of the plants which are responsible for making the vast majority of food within the plant during a process called photosynthesis. Many gardeners are more interested in leaf coloration purely because of its attractiveness and many houseplants fall into this category.

There are the colourful *Coleus blumei* plants, for example. Their ornamental, nettle-like leaves are all shades of green, yellow, red and maroon. Next to the geranium the *Coleus* is probably the most popular window plant. But why are the leaves not all green?

There are many pigments in plants apart from chlorophyll (that provides the green colour), carotenoids for example. As the name suggests this gives carrot roots their orange colour along with tomato fruits and wall-flower – *Cheiranthus* – petals too. Red, blue and violet colours are made by chemicals called anthocyanins. The first *Coleus blumei* plant was collected in Java in 1851 and this is the clue to its unique leaf pattern.

Coleus is used to surviving in the dim conditions prevailing on the ground of the Javan tropical forest. The job of the non-green plant pigments is to collect any light that is available and pass its energy on to the rest of the plant.

Other pigments are used for flower colour, anthoxanthins are found in white and yellow flowers for example. Here their job is to attract insects. But of course the carotenoids and anthocyanins play their part in flower colour too as well as fruit, seed, stem and leaf colour. In some very bright conditions these chemicals may protect the delicate plant tissues beneath.

Roots have two jobs. First, they have to anchor the plant and secondly they have to take in all the water and mineral foods needed by the plant. Stems on the other hand have two other functions. They need to support the leaves in the best place for photosynthesis to occur and also transport water, hormones and other materials up and down the plant. Leaves, roots and stems will be considered later in terms of their normal structure, the way they can be modified and the consequences all of this has for gardeners.

HOW IT ALL BEGAN

The geologists who study the formation and development of the earth, tell us that people – as we know them – appeared about 100,000 years ago. Although this might seem like a long time, it is a mere twinkle when compared with the age of the earth which is thought to be about 4,600 million years old. Where do the flowers fit into this time-scale?

Fossil plants, those which have fallen into primeval muds and been rapidly buried, are of various types. Sometimes the original plant becomes impregnated with rock which hardens to petrify the specimen. Otherwise the only form of evidence is an imprint of a leaf, stem or root. Unfortunately these plant parts may become separated and be named independently. So if you think it is bad enough trying to deal with two or three Latin names for each modern-day plant imagine trying to learn a name for the leaf, root, stem, seed and flower of the same plant! The oldest fossil of a true flowering plant was found in Colorado, USA and dated at about 65 million years old.

The early ancestors of flowering plants were around up to 136 million years ago. That makes them contemporaries of many of the dinosaurs. Since then the life and times of the flowers has been one great success story. They are to be found as far north as 83°N where the Arctic willow (*Salix arctica*) survives and as far south as Antarctica where the carnation (*Colobanthus crassifolius*) flowers.

Mountaineers have often been amazed to find flowers above 20,000 ft (6,135 m) above sea level. Alpine plants like *Stellaria decumbens* have been seen in the rarified air of the Himalayas and they are by no means alone.

If that seems astounding, what about the Cornthwaite Tree in Victoria, Australia. This *Eucalyptus regnans* was recorded as 375 ft (114 m) tall. A European chestnut (*Castanea sativa*) on Mount Etna in Sicily, was said to be 167 ft (51 m) in circumference.

Probably the worst enemy of the gardener is the weed, that unwanted plant which grows faster than any other in the garden. Imagine the problems of maintaining a water garden filled with *Salvinia molesta*. This nonflowering fern, originally from South America, was detected in the Kariba Lake in Zimbabwe, in 1959 and within four years had choked an area of 387 sq miles (1,000 km²).

The speed, or slowness, of flower growth is also a subject worth pondering. Bamboo – a grass – and therefore a flowering plant, is one of the fastest: a specimen of *Albizzia falcataria* grown in Malaysia reached 100 ft (30 m) in just over one year.

Even trees can grow at a remarkable rate. A *Eucalyptus regnans* has been known to grow to the height mentioned earlier in just seven years. On the other hand, the very rare *Puja raimondii* is said to take 150 years to flower, after which it dies. If length is a measure of flowering plant success then how about *Philodendrons*, literally translated as 'tree lovers', which reach up to 300 ft (92 m) in cultivation? One cannot help but wonder what length these plants reach in their natural home, the tropical rainforest and sub-tropical forest of South America.

Meanwhile, that extraordinary plant family, the orchids, show too the same variety of form as seen in the flowering plants taken as a whole. The largest is a Malaysian species called *Grammatophyllum speciosum* which can reach 25 ft (8 m). As far as orchid flower size is concerned, a plant by the magnificent name of *Phragmipedium caudatum* of tropical America has petals 18 in (45 cm) across.

Whilst *Grammatophyllum speciosum* is the tallest free-standing orchid, others rely on trees to help them reach the sunlight. In the rain forest of Queensland, Australia lives *Galcola foliate* which uses other vegetation to reach up to a height of 49 ft (15 m). At the other end of the scale is a miniature Australian plant which bravely bears the name of *Bulbophyllum minutissimum*. This is just one of the contenders for the title 'world's smallest orchid' plant but there is little doubt as to the smallest orchid flower. A magnifying glass would be needed to see the blooms of *Stelis graminea* – they are less than 0.04 in (1 mm) long.

Lastly, how much would you pay for an orchid? A *Cymbidium* orchid, cultivar 'Rosanna Pinkie', was sold for $4,500 (£1,600) in the United States of America in 1952.

CONIFERS – THE GYMNOSPERMS

Long before the flowering plants first put their roots into the earth the conifers and their relations appeared. Strictly speaking this group are called the Gymnosperms, those that bear 'naked seeds', usually in cones (Figure 2.2). About 280 million years ago, 144 million years before flowers appeared, the Gymnosperms made their entrance. They never flourished like the flowering plants, and today only about 700 species of conifer-like plants are to be found.

The tall redwoods have been mentioned before in terms of their Latin name but they are massive too. Take the 'General Sherman' redwood from California whose Latin name is *Sequoia giganteum*. Although this stands a mere 272 ft (83 m) tall it has a girth of 79 ft (24 m). This tree alone has enough wood to make over five million matchsticks.

Not only are conifers the tallest and largest living

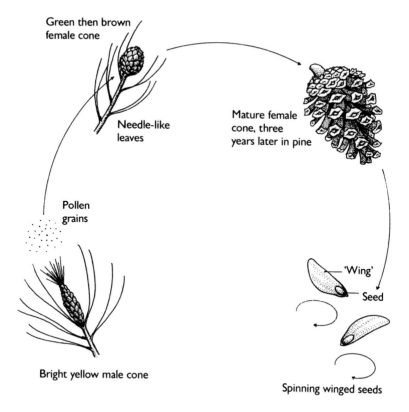

Green then brown
female cone

Needle-like
leaves

Mature female
cone, three
years later in pine

Pollen
grains

'Wing'

Seed

Bright yellow male cone

Spinning winged seeds

Figure 2.2 The Life Cycle of Conifers

things found on earth, they also stake a claim for the
oldest living thing too. A California bristlecone pine,
Pinus aristata, is estimated to be over 4,600 years old.
Apparently they have the potential to reach 5,500 years,
yet the redwoods could potentially live for 6,000 years.

What do all the conifers have in common? Well, they
all share the same kind of life cycle for a start. Unlike
most flowers, which contain both the male and female
reproductive parts, conifers separate these into two
different kinds of cone, which are found on the same tree
(Figure 2.2). In the spring, male pollen grains, like fine
specks of yellow dust, are swept into the air by winds
and a few of these specks will settle on the brown female
cones. The development of seeds takes a long time, three
years in pines, but when dry weather opens the mature
female cones, the winged seeds are revealed which spin
as they fall.

Gardeners often have difficulty germinating conifer
seeds and this is usually because they require the cold of
at least one winter to start them into growth. Gardeners

can put the seeds into some sharp sand in a pot buried in the garden over winter and take them out in the spring to germinate in potting compost. An alternative is to place seeds in a polythene bag, seal it up and place it at the bottom of a refrigerator for three months. After this, a sample of seeds can be sown to test if they are ready to come out yet and this process can be repeated until they are.

Apart from their life style most of the conifers also share needle-like leaves, usually grow upright and all produce resin. It is this resin that gives conifers that characteristic smell and sticky appearance whenever a leaf, twig or branch is removed. It is carried in special resin canals within the tree and is thought to protect the tree by sealing any wounds, and also by making the plant unpalatable to a large range of animal pests and uninhabitable to many plant diseases.

Not all conifers are evergreen and retain their leaves throughout the year, some, like the larch (*Larix*) for example, lose their leaves in the autumn and winter in order to cut down on water requirements. The deciduous habit was one used more frequently by flowering plants, to free them from the need to live in moist situations.

Two other groups are usually included in the Gymnosperm category, they are the yews (*Taxus* species) and Maidenhair tree (*Ginkgo biloba*). Yews have long been thought to possess a magical aura. It is certainly true that every part of the tree apart from the red flesh of the fruits is highly poisonous and this may have given rise to such legends. Male and female flowers are found on separate trees.

Ginkgo trees are deciduous with fan-shaped leaves reminiscent of the maidenhair fern (*Adiantum*) and which turn golden in the autumn. They produce green plum-shaped fruits which ripen to a rancid yellow. Clearly these two types of plant have little in common with the other cone-bearing conifers but since these plants have more in common with one another than any other plants they seem destined to stay put in the Gymnosperms for a while yet.

The Choice of Conifers

The extraordinary variation in conifer texture and colour has captivated the minds of gardeners for generations. As a result many cultivars have been developed and varieties collected to enrich the coniferous tapestry.

Added to this choice, conifers generally thrive in the poorest soils. Some like nothing better than enduring the shallowest of rocky soils. Of course the better the conditions provided by the gardener, the better the growth of the conifers. Most do best in damp, slightly acidic soils but there are others that grow well enough in the dry alkaline soils of limestone and chalk areas. Cedars (*Cedrus*), some junipers (*Juniperus*) and the yews (*Taxus*) can be included in this useful category.

The uses of conifers in gardens are manifold. No garden design is complete without a selection of these plants. The taller conifers can be used to provide shelter in the form of hedges or as single specimens; when the deciduous specimens lose their leaves the conifer needles remain to give solidity and, usually, a special winter colour too.

Take the Leyland cypress (*Cupressocyparis* × *leylandii*) for example. This is a hybrid created by a cross between the Monterey cypress (*Cupressus macrocarpa*) and Nootka cypress (*Chamaecyparis nootkatensis*). They can reach 30 ft (9 m) tall in ten years and eventually 50 ft (16 m) tall with a spread of 15 ft (5 m). It is one of the most widely used conifers for hedging and screening, growing over 3 ft (1 m) a year when established. It is very adaptable as far as climate and soil type are concerned, even tolerating coastal areas which suffer the effects of sea spray.

Several cultivars are available. 'Robinson's Gold' has bright yellow new growth, 'Haggerston Grey' has shoots with dark grey-green scales and rarely produces cones, 'Leighton Green' has sprays of rich green; but many favour 'Castlewellan Gold' which is quite compact in habit but its real bonus lies in its colour. In summer the foliage is golden yellow and in winter a more sulphur yellow colour is displayed.

Otherwise there are cedars (*Cedrus*), cypresses (*Chamaecyparis* and *Cupressus*), spruces (*Picea*), pines (*Pinus*) and the arbor-vitae (*Thuja*) to brighten up the garden on a large scale.

In these days when gardens are getting smaller and some people have no more than a patio, balcony or window-box it is comforting to know that the conifers can help provide interest and colour throughout the year. Many genera of conifers have dwarf or very slow-growing forms which are useful in larger gardens too. Rock gardens, island beds, borders, sink gardens, lawns and even pots can all benefit from dwarf conifers.

If cool conditions are provided they may even be taken indoors for short periods although it must be emphasised that these plants are identical to their larger relatives with respect to hardiness and cultural requirements.

There are firs (*Abies*), cypresses (*Chamaecyparis*, *Cupressocyparis* and *Cupressus*), junipers (*Juniperus*), Japanese cedars (*Cryptomeria*), spruces (*Picea*), pines (*Pinus*), coast redwoods (*Sequoia sempervirens*), yews (*Taxus*) and arborvitae (*Thuja*). It really is a case of being spoilt for choice.

Junipers are a case in point. These conifers can be green, blue, grey and yellow. Sometimes they grow along the ground (are prostrate), or hold themselves clear of the soil as they spread (are semi-prostrate) or grow upright and erect as broad blades or narrow columns. Some catalogues offer over 60 types of dwarf conifer so perhaps there is no excuse for any gardener omitting the junipers from their garden no matter how small it may be. Clearly the conifers, like the flowering plants, are a gardening success story – but where do the ferns fit into this story?

FERNS

There are up to 10,000 species of fern in the world today. They belong to a group of plants called the Pteridophytes which is translated from the Greek for 'feather leaf'. Ferns range in size from floating species the size of a drawing pin-head, like *Azolla caroliniana*, to the tree ferns of Pacific islands which may reach up to 60 ft (18 m) tall, like *Alsophila excelsa* of Norfolk Island. But what is it that makes a fern, a fern?

Ferns have a unique life cycle (Figure 2.3) which starts with the leaf-like structure we call a frond. Beneath the pinnae that make up the frond are tiny capsules called sori which bear spores. When ripe these spores are carried by wind currents. Some will find ideal conditions to germinate – warm, moist and shady.

From these germinating spores little sexual plants develop and when these mature reproduction takes place. Only when very wet conditions exist can the male cells swim – yes, swim – across the sexual plants to fertilise the female cells. This part of the life cycle ties the ferns to wet places and has done since the days 395 million years ago when they first appeared, that is 115 million years before the conifers and 259 million years before the first flowers appeared. After fertilisation a frond develops out of the plant and after a short while the process begins again.

The number of ferns of use to gardeners is immense. There are bird's nest ferns (*Asplenium nidus*) which resemble bright green shuttlecocks, maidenhair ferns (*Adiantum capillus-veneris*) with their light green triangular

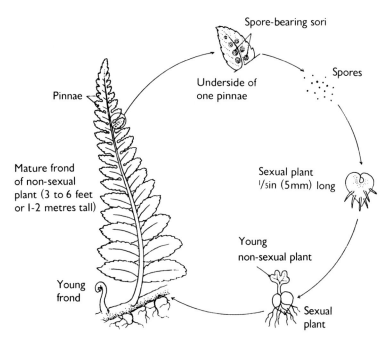

Figure 2.3 The Life of a Fern

fronds on black stalks and ostrich feather (*Matteuccia struthiopteris*), royal (*Osmunda regalis*), staghorn (*Platycerium* species), lady (*Athyrium filix-femina*), male (*Dryopteris filix-mas*) and ribbon (*Pteris cretica*) ferns too.

Gardeners can make use of their knowledge of the fern life cycle in order to produce more specimens for practically no cost. When the fronds have matured spores will begin to be released from the sori beneath (see Figure 2.3).

If a mature frond is placed on a clean white sheet of paper in a dry, still place the dust-like spores will become detached and leave their 'fingerprint' on the paper.

Using sieved compost made up of equal parts coarse sand, leaf-mould or peat and loam, fill a seed pan and pour boiling water over it to kill any unwanted spores already on the pan or in the mix. When cool cover with a clean piece of glass to exclude any other spores that might be in the air and are likely to contaminate the mixture.

Using the tip of a dry brush or knife pick up a small number of spores and shake them as evenly as possible over the surface of the compost. Cover up with a glass sheet as soon as possible and place the seed pad in a shady place, perhaps under the bench of a greenhouse. If the spores were obtained from a fern requiring heat during cultivation then heat will be needed now.

Usually after one to three months later the minute sexual plants will start to appear (see Figure 2.3) like a green film on the surface. Do not remove the glass, otherwise contamination will strike, instead stand the seed pan in water at intervals to give the ferns an appropriate amount of water.

When they are large enough to prick off into pans make sure the humidity stays high as drying out could be disastrous. After a while the fern plants will be large enough to pot on into single pots. Once again, if the ferns will need heat when mature they will need it now. Only when the ferns are appreciated in terms of their life style can they be cared for. When composts get too wet the mosses invade.

MOSSES

Unfortunately for mosses they are regarded by gardeners only as a menace, as those plants which are found in the lawn and on flowerpots when least expected and wanted even less. To understand why they seemingly 'suddenly' appear, it is necessary to delve into their private lives.

Moss plants first appeared on earth about 430 million years ago. They were among the first plants to invade the land from the seas and are still tied to the water for their existence.

They belong to a group of plants called the Bryophytes – meaning 'moss plants' – which also contains the liverworts, peculiar green objects with no proper stems or leaves. The normal moss plant to be found in the garden has small leaves which wrap around the stem at their base (Figure 2.4). It has small root-like structures which anchor the moss and take in food and water from the soil. This is the sexual part of the life cycle which contains the male and female parts.

When the plant is mature and wet conditions abound the male sperm cells swim to fertilise the female eggs. As a result out grows the familiar non-sexual stalk with a container or capsule at the end which is filled with spores.

Later, when the spores are properly developed and the weather is dry, off drops the cap – and the spores are released.

Any spores which settle in the wet conditions needed will germinate to produce a new generation of sexual

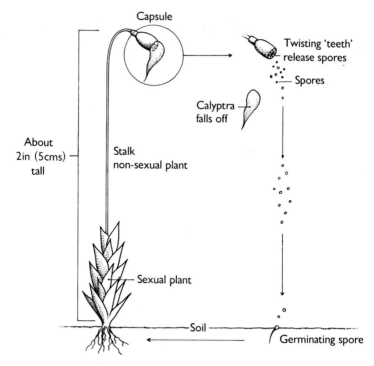

Capsule

Twisting 'teeth'
release spores

Spores

Calyptra
falls off

About
2in (5cms)
tall

Stalk
non-sexual plant

Sexual plant

Soil

Germinating spore

Figure 2.4 The Life of a Moss

moss plants. Which explains why moss plants are always found in wet places; the surface of over-wet compost, the top of a poorly drained lawn, and so on. In spite of their requirement for soggy wet places mosses are difficult to remove because they easily break up into small fragments each of which can regenerate into complete new plants. Secondly, the air is filled with moss spores so even if mosses are removed, if the area is not dried out they are very likely to return. The answer is to make areas uninhabitable to mosses by keeping them well drained. Addition of sharp sand to lawns and reduction of watering to house plants are just two ways of discouraging them.

Mosses and ferns are doomed to dwell in only the dampest places on earth. The conifers were able to inhabit drier land but it was the flowering plants that were to inherit the horticultural crown. Their varied life styles all have one common character and that is the most obvious and important one – the flower. Gardeners have more often introduced new plants into the garden for their flowers than any other character they might incidently possess. It is fitting, then, that flowers will be the next subject in this voyage of discovery.

3 Flower Power

CLASSIFICATION

Since there are about a quarter of a million different species of flowering plants on earth the search to classify them into easily recognisable groups has been long and thorough.

Perhaps the easiest and most convenient way to subdivide the flowers is to decide whether they are 'monocots' or 'dicots'. **Monocots**, or more precisely the monocotyledonous flowering plants, are those which have leaf veins that run parallel to one another, like railway lines. Also their flower parts (see Figure 2.1 and 3.1), such as petals and stamens, are in multiples of three. When monocot seeds germinate they do so using one cotyledon or seed leaf. The inside arrangement or anatomy of monocotyledons is also different to those of dicots.

If you can recognise some of these features it is not surprising because many garden plants share these characteristics. All the commonly occurring plants that use bulbs in which to store their food are monocots, so daffodils (*Narcissus* species) and tulips (*Tulipa* species) are just two monocots along with the orchids (about 20,000 species), bromeliads (about 1,400 species), palms (like the date palms, *Phoenix dactylifera*), *Crocuses* (over 70 species) and *Gladioli* (over 300 species), onions (*Allium* species) and many more besides including the grasses, whether ornamental or just successful weeds.

All the other flowering plants are called **dicots** or dicotyledonous plants (Figure 3.1). Dicots have leaf veins that spread out and interconnect with one another, like the lines on the palms of your hands, in so-called net venation. Their flowers have parts in multiples of fours or fives. When dicots germinate their seeds use two seed leaves rather than one and their plant anatomy is based on a different pattern. The number of dicots is hard to envisage. *Achillea, Agrostemma, Alyssum, Anchusa, Anemone, Anthemis, Aquilegia, Ageratum, Amaranthus* and *Arctotis* species are just some of the dicots which can be grown from seed these days.

Another way of classifying flowering plants – and

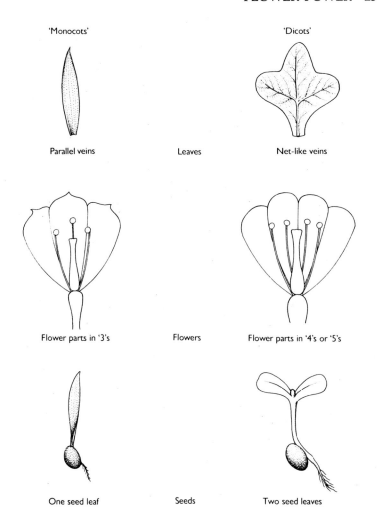

'Monocots'   'Dicots'

Parallel veins   Leaves   Net-like veins

Flower parts in '3's   Flowers   Flower parts in '4's or '5's

One seed leaf   Seeds   Two seed leaves

Figure 3.1 Monocots and Dicots

other plants for that matter – is by the length of their life cycles. Some plants can complete their life span in less than one growing season (Figure 3.2). Weeds, those eternal adversaries of the gardener, are extremely good at shortening their lives so as to produce as many offspring as possible.

Take groundsel (*Senecio vulgaris*) for example. From a minute seed on the end of a fluffy 'parachute', which floats through the air like a botanical Peter Pan and germinates wherever it can to produce more seed-producing adult plants, takes a mere five weeks. Such plants are called **ephemerals**. Because of the numerous seeds produced and the rapidity by which seeds germin-

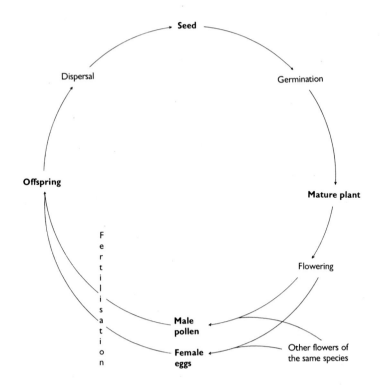

Figure 3.2 The Flower Life Story. The length of this life cycle determines whether the plant is an ephemeral (weeks), annual (one growing season), biennial (two growing seasons) or perennial (more than two growing seasons)

ate, grow, flower and produce in turn their own seeds the number of offspring produced each year is phenomenal. Each parent groundsel plant is capable of producing up to 1,000 million descendants each year. No wonder gardeners are forever weeding!

Gardeners are more familiar with the term **annual plants**. These complete their lives during one growing season, not normally a full year because of the low winter temperatures which prevent growth or germination. Annuals can be subdivided into hardy and half-hardy annual plants for the guidance of gardeners who practise their art in areas where frost is a hazard. The climate map given in Figure 1.1 shows that frost might be expected in any of the zones, but the chances of its happening increase as the zone number decreases, that is, Zone 9 has a greater chance of frost than Zone 10, and so on.

Hardy annual plant species like *Anchusa, Asperula, Bartonia, Calendula, Calliopsis* and *Campanula*, and so on are sown in the spring – perhaps March or April – because they will tolerate frost conditions.

Half-hardy annuals like the species *Ageratum Calceolaria, Cineraria, Dianthus, Kochia* and *Lobelia* cannot stand frost. They can be sown outside but only when the greatest danger of frost has gone, usually in May and June. If an earlier start is wanted the half-hardy annual seeds can be sown earlier in protected places. In a cold greenhouse or frame the seeds can be sown in March or April, in a heated greenhouse or frame a half-hardy annual can be sown any time between January and April.

Biennials come next, they complete their lives in two years. The pattern is to germinate from seed, grow and develop in the first year and then flower and produce seed in the second year. Canterbury bells (*Campanula medium*) and foxgloves (*Digitalis* species) are just two biennial flowers; but what is most interesting is that many vegetables fall into this category too.

Cabbages (*Brassica oleracea capitata*), beetroots (*Beta vulgaris conditiva*), turnips (*Brassica rapa*) and carrots (*Daucus carota*) are just some of the biennial vegetables available to the gardener, but usually they are picked in their first year after germination when they have grown but not flowered. Many biennials, like carrots, make a food store in the root during the first year and before the plant gets the chance to use the food for flower and seed production, we pick it.

Some biennials, like lettuce (*Lactuca sativa*) 'bolt', that is, they flower when least expected. What happens is this: in drought conditions or in poor soils where the plants might not make it to the second year the biennial switches into 'overdrive' and flowers prematurely.

Unfortunately for the gardener this not only means that energy normally used for crop production goes into seed formation instead but also that the shape of the plant changes too. The familiar rosette, where leaves are arranged like the petals of a flower, changes to a tall spire – a 3 ft (1 m) tall lettuce-spire is of little use to the gardener.

Perennials are any plants that take more than three growing seasons to complete their lives. It applies to the familiar herbaceous plants, those that have no woody growth above soil level and die down in frosty conditions, like Anemone, Lily of the Valley (*Convallaria majalis*), *Delphinium, Astilbe, Artemisia, Hosta* and many others besides including herbs like parsley (*Petroselinum crispum*).

Interestingly, many perennials are treated as biennials because they lose their form and ability to produce flowers freely after a couple of years. Sweet Williams

(*Dianthus barbatus*) and Wallflowers (*Cheiranthus* species) are two perennials usually grown over two years.

Do not forget that the deciduous and evergreen flowering trees and shrubs are all perennials too, including the conifers. And then there are the roses, *Rhododendron, Spiraea, Forsythia, Magnolia, Buddleia, Potentilla,* apple (*Malus*), pear (*Pyrus communis*), *Clematis, Hydrangea,* Dogwood (*Cornus*), maple (*Acer*), oak (*Quercus*), lilac (*Syringa*), *Wisteria* species and many, many more.

In horticultural shows a distinction is often drawn between the hardy perennials and those that will not survive life in cooler areas like Zones 6, 7 and 8 on figure 1.2. In truth they will all be perennials of course and if given sufficient heat would survive much longer than their unprotected counterparts.

Even in similar types of crops a range of life spans and cultivation techniques are used. Take beans for example. Broad bean (*Vicia faba*) is a hardy, easily grown annual. The French, dwarf or kidney bean (*Phaseolus vulgaris*) is best regarded as a half-hardy annual to be sown later in the spring if frost is likely, usually between April and May.

The runner bean (*Phaseolus coccineus*) is a perennial but since it is tender in areas where frosts are likely (anywhere except in Zone 10), it is sown outside in mid-April and has until October or November to germinate, grow, flower and produce a crop; quite a remarkable plant.

Some plants, which live for more than one season, also die after flowering. Many of these once-fruiting or monocarpic type of plants produce a rosette of leaves until the time they flower, fruit and die. *Billbergia, Vriesea, Agave, Saxifraga* and *Sempervivum* species all fall into this category. It must be a sad thought that a white plume-like flowerhead on a fine five-year-old specimen of *Saxifraga longifolia* signals the doom of the plant. Worst still, perhaps tragic, is the production of 10 ft (3 m) spikes of flowers on 20 ft (6 m) flower stalks by 50-year-old century plants (*Agave americana*). What a poignant 'swan song', that such a magnificent sight signals the death of the plant.

FAMILIES OF FLOWERS

Once the flowering plant has been described, be it monocot or dicot, hardy or tender, annual, biennial or perennial, it is usually placed in a family.

Botanists find that it is very convenient to represent the structure of a flower symbolically, in a formula. Working from the outside of the flower (see Figure 2.1), each part is given a letter – K for all the sepals composing the calyx, C for the petals making up the corolla, A for the male stamens of the androecium and G for the segments or carpels of the pistil or gynaecium. Then each part is given a figure relating to the number of constituents.

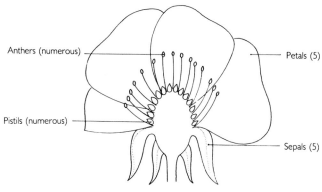

Anthers (numerous)

Petals (5)

Pistils (numerous)

Sepals (5)

Remember: K5 C5 A∞ G∞

Figure 3.3 Rosaceae Flower Structure

So, to take an example, all the flowers which belong to the rose family, the *Rosaceae*, have the basic structure K5 C5 A∞ G∞ (Figure 3.3). It does not matter whether a rose, strawberry (*Fragaria* × *ananassa*), raspberry or blackberry (both *Rubus* species), or pear (*Pyrus communis*) is examined. The basic structure will be 5 sepals, 5 petals and numerous stamens and pistils.

Another example would be the *Papilionaceae* family (sometimes called the *Fabaceae*). This group includes the lupins (*Lupinus* species), sweet peas (*Lathyrus* species), broad bean, gorse and broom (*Genista* and *Cytisus* species), clover (*Trifolium* species) and garden pea (*Pisum sativum*).

Their secret formula is K(5) C5 A(5 + 5) G 1 (Figure 3.4). This has all the normal components plus two additions. There are 5 sepals and the brackets indicate that they are fused together to make a calyx. There are 5 separate petals but the stamens are in two sets of 5, one surrounding the other. There is only one carpel, gynaecium, and the line beneath the figure indicates the structure is superior, that is, it sits on top of the point where the sepals and petals are attached to the flower.

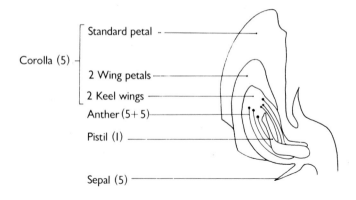

Corolla (5)
- Standard petal
- 2 Wing petals
- 2 Keel wings
Anther (5+ 5)
Pistil (I)
Sepal (5)

Remember: K(5) C5 A (5+5) G̲I̲

Figure 3.4 Papilionaceae Flower Structure

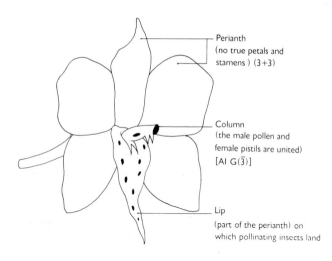

Perianth
(no true petals and
stamens) (3+3)

Column
(the male pollen and
female pistils are united)
[AI G($\overline{3}$)]

Lip
(part of the perianth) on
which pollinating insects land

Remember: P3+3 AI G($\overline{3}$)

Figure 3.5 Orchidaceae Flower Structure

The last important feature of this type of flower is that it is not circular but flattened. This will have important consequences for the flower when it wants to complete reproduction.

Orchids (*Orchidaceae*) show extreme flower structure. Their general formula is P3 + 3 A1 G($\overline{3}$) (Figure 3.5). The numbers indicate that it is a monocot. The use of P instead of C and K means that no true sepals and petals can be distinguished, so the word perianth is used. The formula indicates that the perianth consists of two rings of 3 structures, one of which is modified into a lip. There is only one stamen which does not carry pollen as in other flowers. The male pollen grains are united into waxy spherical structures called pollinia. The floral sexual organs are gathered together into one structure called a column. The three carpels are fused together and buried deep in the flower stalk or receptacle.

Lastly, let us turn to the grasses (*Gramineae*) which are possibly the most important plant family as they have not only produced suitable plants for lawns but also feed millions of people in the form of cereals like wheat, oats and rice. It is with amazement that some gardeners discover that grasses are flowering plants. The fact that all grasses have parallel leaf veins indicates that they are monocots, but where are the flowers? These are simple structures and because of their variety a floral formula is impossible.

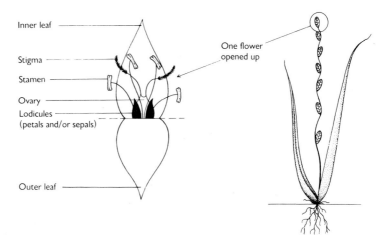

Figure 3.6 The Flower Structure of Grasses

Grass petals and sepals are virtually non-existent and called lodicules (Figure 3.6). The stamens are large and pendulous whereas the ovary contains a single ovule. Perennial rye grass (*Lolium perenne*) is the familiar grass whose flower stalks seem to defy the sharpest of lawn mower blades. Fortunately dwarf strains are now available which means that this hard-wearing grass is now welcomed in lawn seed mixture.

THE GENETICS OF POLLINATION

Whereas the mosses and ferns discussed earlier depend on external water for the male cells to swim in in order to fertilise the female eggs, the conifers and better still the flowering plants have solved this problem.

Flowering plants wrap their eggs under several layers of tissue to protect them from drying out. The ovary surrounds the ovule and the ovule surrounds the ovum (or egg) rather like wooden Russian dolls surround one another. This 'double wrapped' seal ensures that as long as the male cells make it to the pistil all should be well.

The next step is pollination, the transfer of pollen grains from male stamens to female pistils. Sometimes flowers can be pollinated by pollen from the same plant. This is called self-pollination and occurs in peas, beans, peaches and nectarines (*Prunus persica*), apricots (*Prunus armeniaca*) and some plums and gages (*Prunus domestica*).

Alternatively, the pollen might have to come from another plant of the same species. Many varieties of apples, pears, sweet cherries (*Prunus avium* varieties) and elderberries (*Sambucus* species) are self-incompatible. This means that several varieties of the same fruit, that flower at the same time, must be grown together so that they can provide one another with pollen and thus cross-pollinate.

Different varieties of fruit flower at different times so it is possible to divide them into pollination groups. All the varieties in any given group open their flowers at the same time. Also those in adjacent groups are useful because in most seasons their flowering periods overlap.

There can be up to seven pollination groups for some fruits like apples and some of these groups may have in excess of 50 varieties. Unfortunately, not all the varieties of the same group can cross-pollinate. This is known to the fruit growers as cross-incompatibility. These varieties are often listed in incompatibility groups and will not set fruit with their own pollen or that of any variety which appears in that group. In the case of pears one incompatibility group is 'Laxton's Progress' 'Seckle', 'Fondante d'Automne', 'Williams' Bon Chretien', 'Precoce de Trevoux' and 'Louis Bonne of Jersey'. Fortunately, these varieties will cross-pollinate with those of another group. So 'Laxton's Progress' will be compatible with others in pear pollination group 3 including 'Roosevelt', 'Conference' and 'Dr Jules Guyot'.

What happens if the wrong pollen grain makes it to the stigma (see Figure 2.1) of an incompatible variety?

Not a lot is the answer! Either it does not germinate or it manages to start growing but never makes it to the fertilisation stage.

Some varieties are not very effective providers of pollen, or pollinators, and one of the reasons for this lies in their chromosomes. Every living thing, including plants, is made of units called cells. Cells may become very specialised, to make petals or leaves for example, but all of them possess identical chromosomes which are minute structures formed within the cells. The chromosomes carry the code which enables cells to do everything they have to do during life.

Put simply most plant cells, like our own, have pairs of chromosomes which when totalled up give the diploid number. Our normal body cells have 46 chromosomes, so 46 is the human diploid number. Broad beans have 12 chromosomes and apples have 34 chromosomes in normal cells, therefore those are their diploid numbers (Figure 3.7).

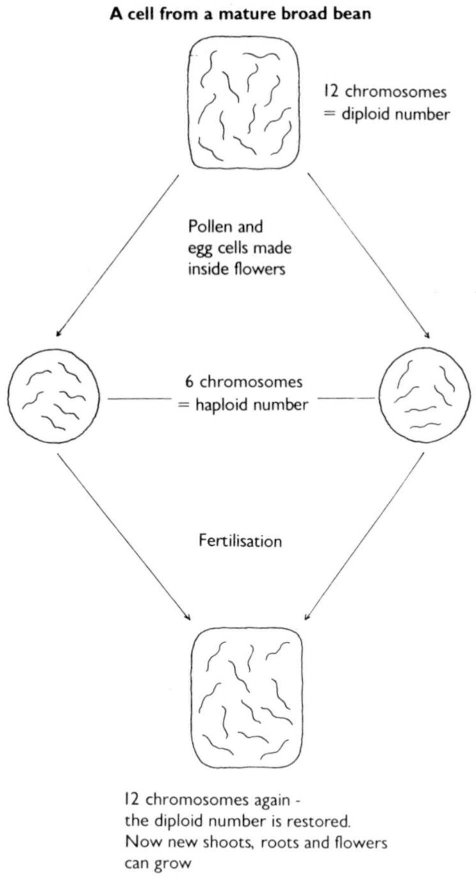

A cell from a mature broad bean

12 chromosomes = diploid number

Pollen and egg cells made inside flowers

6 chromosomes = haploid number

Fertilisation

12 chromosomes again - the diploid number is restored. Now new shoots, roots and flowers can grow

Figure 3.7 Broad Bean Chromosomes

In order to make sex cells the diploid number is halved. Humans produce eggs and sperm with 23 chromosomes so that when they fuse the normal 46 chromosome number is resumed. Likewise the broad bean will make eggs – or ova – and pollen grains with 6 chromosomes. When fertilisation is complete the broad bean diploid number is made again.

Returning to apples and pears, some of these varieties are known as triploids. This means that they have $1\frac{1}{2}$ times the normal diploid number, or 3 times the haploid number, whichever way you prefer to look at it. Triploid apples include 'Bramleys seedling' and triploid pears include 'Merton Pride'. Although they can produce fruit they have great difficulty producing viable pollen. Naturally, if there are two diploid varieties growing nearby they will be able to pollinate each other as well as the triploid variety, assuming they flower at the same time of course!

The problems of a would-be apple and pear grower are not finished yet, however. Some varieties are not good at pollination because they produce such small amounts of pollen. The 'Marguerite Marillat' pear is such an example. Others cannot be relied upon because they flower biennially or irregularly like 'Fortune', 'Wagener' and 'Superb (Laxtons)' apples. It has to be said, though, that the gardener might well wish to tolerate the irregular crops in order to obtain well-flavoured fruit, particularly if more regularly cropping varieties are grown too.

POLLINATION

There is no point in possessing pretty flowers unless they work well enough for seed production to occur. It would be like owning the shell of a Rolls-Royce car without the engine.

In order to bring about seed formation the flowers must ensure pollination, that is the transfer of pollen from flower to flower. This is brought about in two main ways. First, the flowers may try to attract animals like insects. They do this by being conspicuous and brightly coloured. Also they offer food in the form of excess pollen, and, maybe, sweet-tasting, energy-rich nectar. The flowers of the *Rosaceae*, *Papilionaceae* and *Orchidaceae* families all fall into this category.

The flowers of the *Papilionaceae* family are specially designed to make sure that insects like bees take pollen from flower to flower. The stigma (see Figure 2.1) is not connected to the keel and when an insect lands on the flower the 'chimney sweep brush' of a stigma sweeps upwards depositing rough and sticky pollen from surrounding stamens on the underside of the insect. At the same time the stigma will pick up pollen grains from other plants that have been deposited on the same insect.

Other flowers, like those of the *Gramineae*, rely on the wind for pollination. As a result there is no need for bright colours, in fact the flowers are small, inconspicuous and green. The petals and sepals are very reduced and may even be absent. On the other hand the stamens may be very long and hang out of the flower to ensure the wind picks the pollen up. The female stigma is often large, branched and feathery in appearance and held out of the flower in order to enable it to catch the pollen carried on the wind. There is no need for nectar or scent in wind-pollinated flowers so they are not found.

It may come as a surprise to find that some plants have flowers which may contain only male stamens or female pistils. If these two types of flower are found on the same plant it is said to be monoecious. Examples are sweet corn (*Zea mays*), hazel (*Corylus* species) and cucumber (*Cucumis sativus*). Equally, the male and female flowers may be found on separate plants which are described as dioecious. Such flowering plants include hollies (*Ilex* species where the variety 'Golden King' is a female tree and 'Silver Queen' is a male tree!), *Pernettya* and *Skimmia*. This is a problem easily overcome in the garden by planting a male plant upwind and near to several female plants.

Once the correct pollen has made the hazardous journey, rather like a human swimming the Atlantic ocean without compass directions, then the next part of the journey is equally hard, like tunnelling from the British Isles to Australia. Successful pollen grains germinate on the sugary layers which lie on the stigma. A pollen tube grows down through the style and down through the ovary towards an ovule. The weak point in the wall of the ovule is a small hole called the micropyle. It is through this micropyle that the pollen tube penetrates. On entry to the ovule a double fertilisation takes place. This is a 'speciality act' performed only by flowering plants. Not only is the egg fertilised but a food store is made by the second fertilisation.

In this way the information from one generation gets passed on to the next. The secret of inheritance was discovered by an Austrian monk by the name of Gregor Mendel.

MENDEL'S THEORY OF INHERITANCE

In 1866 Abbé Mendel published his theory of inheritance which was based on work with peas in the monastery garden. Tragically Mendel never had his work recognised in his lifetime. He died in 1884 but his work was not rediscovered until 1900.

How fortunate it was that he chose to work with the pea. These plants have seven clear-cut characteristics which can be followed generation to generation; seed form (round or wrinkled); colour of reserve food in the seed leaves (yellow or green cotyledons); ripe pod form (inflated,/smooth or constricted/wrinkled); seed coat and flower colour (whitish seeds/white flowers or greyish seeds/purple flowers); colour of unripe pods (green or yellow); flower position (at ends or sides of stems); and stem length (tall or dwarf).

Take pea plant height for example. Mendel knew, as we know today, that peas are either tall (6-9 ft, 2-2.5 m) or dwarf (8-16 in, 0.2-0.4 m). He decided to cross pure-breeding tall and dwarf varieties and see the effects on the offspring. Would they be tall, dwarf, medium-sized or a mixture? (Figure 3.8).

Garden peas normally self-pollinate so this had to be prevented. He decided that one parent, say tall plants,

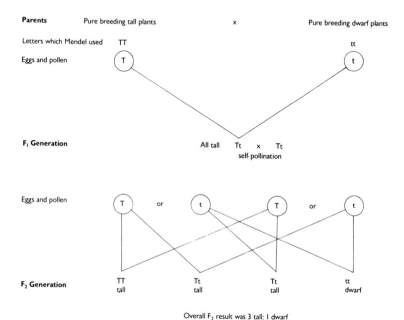

Figure 3.8 Mendel's Pea Breeding Experiment

should provide pollen and these flowers would be allowed to ripen normally. The other parent plant flowers, of the dwarf plants, would be emasculated, that is before the flower opened it would be cut open and the unripe, pollen-providing stamens would be removed before they tried to fertilise that flower.

Of course pollen from other plants could have already been shed into the air so to prevent these grains from landing on the emasculated flowers a little muslin bag was tied around each treated flower.

When the pollen from the chosen plants was ripe their flowers were picked and the stamens rubbed on the stigma of the other parent flower. If tall plants were selected for male, pollen, parents and dwarf plants for female, pistil, parents then the process was reversed next time to make sure that any results obtained were only due to genetic reasons.

The peas were allowed to ripen, then harvested and sown the following year. To his great surprise the cross of tall and dwarf parents produced all tall offspring, known as the first filial generation or F_1.

Even more astounding were the results obtained from allowing all the F_1 generation to self-pollinate. The second generation, or F_2, were sown and consisted of 787 tall plants and 277 dwarf plants. This was approximately a 3 to 1 ratio.

Mendel said the tall factor must be dominant to dwarf since it hides the dwarfness in the F_1. The dwarf factor appears to be hidden in the first generation but reappears in the second. Mendel said dwarf was recessive.

What about the other six characters? Round seeds, yellow seed leaves, inflated and smooth ripe pods, greyish seeds with purple flowers, green unripe pods and flowers at the side rather than the tip of stems were all dominant to their counterparts. They all appeared in the F_1 generation and showed the same 3 to 1 ratio in the F_2.

Mendel had discovered a fundamental law of nature. Genetic crosses followed mathematical rules. Mendel went on to use letters to express his conclusions. He used capital letters for dominant factors and lower case letters for recessive factors (see Figure 3.8). Secondly, he realised that there must be a pair of factors in each parent plant and only one factor in pollen grains so that when the latter combine during fertilisation the double, or diploid, number is restored. So TT and tt represented pure-breeding tall and dwarf plants respectively.

When the parents made pollen grains and eggs each of

these could only carry a single factor. So if the tall parent plants provided pollen each pollen grain would carry a single T factor. Equally if dwarf parent plants were used to provide eggs, each of these would contain a single t factor.

During fertilisation the T and t factors would combine and when the egg matured inside a seed and this seed was sown the resulting plant would be tall because T is dominant to t. Notice that although these tall F_1 plants look like their tall parent they carry a different combination of factors.

When these F_1 plants were allowed to self-pollinate their pollen grains and eggs could carry either a T or t factor. A T or t pollen grain could combine with a T or t egg so four combinations of factors could be made; TT, Tt, tT and tt. The first three plants would contain at least one dominant T factor and so they would be tall peas. The last combination has two recessive t factors and so would be dwarf. The 3 to 1 ratio is explained. There was no mixing or blending of the factors and for the first time breeding was no longer trial and error but an exact science which could often predict results.

Many seed catalogues carry glorious descriptions of so-called F_1 hybrids. From the previous discussion of breeding it will become obvious that an F_1 hybrid is the product of breeding two pure-breeding parental lines. Also the F_1 plants may look like one of the parents but will have a different mixture of factors or genetic material. Often F_1 hybrids may show extra vigour, hardiness, resistance to disease, more uniform and heavier fruiting and more profuse flowering. This hybrid vigour declines in subsequent generations so a repetition of the original cross has to be made.

Half-hardy F_1 annuals are now bountiful, seed catalogues include *Begonia, Ageratum, Antirrhinum, Calceolaria*, carnations and pinks (*Dianthus*), geraniums (*Pelargonium × hortorum*), *Impatiens*, African-French marigolds (*Tagetes*), monkey flowers (*Mimulus*), flowering tobacco (*Nicotiana*), *Petunia*, sun plants (*Portulaca*) and *Zinnia*.

Vegetables have shown the F_1 fashion too. Calabrese (*Brassica oleracea botrytis*), cabbage (*Brassica oleracea capitata*), Brussels sprouts (*Brassica oleracea gemmifera*), peppers (*Capsicum*), carrots, chicory (*Chichorium intybus*), cucumbers, marrows (*Cucurbita pepo ovifera*), melons (*Cucurmis melo*), onions (*Allium cepa*), pumpkins (*Cucurbita maxima* and *C. moschata*), sweet corn and tomato.

Since the production of F_1 seeds is costly in terms of

labour this is reflected in the price. Trying to recoup the cost by keeping seeds from F_1 plants after they have flowered and fruited in order to use these the following seasons is a waste of time. The F_2 generation is such a mixture of genetic material that the plants will vary in all the factors sought in the F_1. They will probably vary in height, flower colour, fruit size and yield, ability to withstand extremes of temperature and disease. As such F_2 seed is of little use to the gardener who wants consistently predictable results.

BREEDING YOUR OWN PLANTS

It is perfectly possible to see new, previously unculti-vated varieties in the wild. Take the Shirley poppies for example. The first was seen by Reverend Wilks amongst other field poppies (*Papaver rhoeas*) in a rough corner of the rectory garden at Shirley in Kent, in the late nineteenth century. He observed that some wild red poppies had white-edged petals, made a note of their location and returned to collect their seeds at the end of the summer.

He sowed these seeds, waited for the plants to flower and then ruthlessly discarded any that showed the normal plain red coloration. Reverend Wilks repeated this sowing, rearing and selection process many times until the famous Shirley poppies were established, showing a range of colours including pinks, white, rose, salmon and crimson.

This selection process is important for any plant breeder too. The garden plants with useful characteristics for hybridisation, whatever they might be, are only of use if some 'eagle-eyed' gardener has noticed those particular plants and labelled them for future use.

The same careful selection of offspring is necessary when doing your own plant breeding. Many plants lend themselves to breeding. Amongst the vegetables that are easily cross-bred are; tomatoes, squash, peppers, cabbage, cucumber, marrow, Brussels sprouts and radish. Flowers which are worth experimenting with are: *Amaryllis, Delphinium, Petunia, Lavatera,* Nasturtium, *Nicotiana, Nemesia, Godetia* and *Primula*.

Ideally a bed of each prospective parent should be established and when they flower they should all be progressively emasculated. The pollen from one parent should be dusted on to the stigma of the other parent. This should be a two-way process so that both sets of parents act as both mother and father.

If pollination has been successful the stigma will blacken and shrivel, petals will fall too. Of course not all the flowers will open at the same time, but as soon as they do carry out cross-pollination.

When the seed pods ripen and dry pick them and place them in a labelled paper bag. These should be stored in a cool dry place. Next season sow these seeds and grow them on as if they were any normal plant. Pay special attention to all the seedlings, no matter how small they may be – often the smallest plants give the best final results.

Try to grow the original parent-type plants somewhere else in the garden and in the new F_1 offspring pull out and destroy any plants that are of no use as parents for the next generation, the F_2. It may well be true that only a few flowers are left but leave these to cross-pollinate amongst themselves and collect the seed as before. Germinate the seed the following season and repeat the process until all the seed sown produces one type of distinct plant. This may take many years and so is not for the gardener who wants quick and predictable results.

All that is happening in plant breeding is a greatly speeded-up version of what would happen if the same parents cross-bred in nature. The advantage, apart from speed, is that if, say, you like the height of the white flowered *Lavatera* 'Mont Blanc' (2 ft, 60 cm) but prefer the deep cerise-pink flower colour of 'Tanagra' it would be possible to select offspring of these that had just the right height and flower colour. On the other hand it is possible to choose a good-flavoured tomato like 'Ailsa Craig' as one parent and the yellow-skinned 'Golden Sunrise' as the other. Perhaps one of the offpsring would be yellow-skinned and of excellent flavour. There really is no limit to the type of experimental breeding that can be done on many of the plants normally found in any garden.

SEED SUCCESS

Part of the success of flowering plants lies in their ability to produce their 'double-wrapped' seeds. Protected by the tough seed coat and ovary wall the fruit can take on a whole range of forms to delight the gardener, either visually like *Cotoneaster* or tastefully like apples and pears.

The ovary wall can dry up to form a nut, as in the walnut (*Juglans regia*), or become fleshy to make a berry. The berries are a widespread occurrence and include gooseberry, cucumber, melon, orange, grape, banana, pomegranate (*Punica granatum*), tomato and date.

Alternatively, a dry, one-seeded fruit called an achene may be formed. Many achenes are usually found within a fruiting head as in the buttercup (*Ranunculus species*) and rose or on the outside of the fleshy fruit as in the strawberry. To add to this complex picture seeds which are enclosed within a hard 'stone' which protects it and which in turn is surrounded by a fleshy pulp are called drupes. Cherries and plums are the simplest form of drupe, but if the flesh-coated seeds are joined together, as in raspberry and blackberry, the correct term is compound drupe.

Although many Australians believe the 'pome' is someone from England!, the gardener should know different. Actually the pome is fleshy fruit which contains a number of seed-containing cells. Apples, pears and many other plants fit into this category.

Obviously the business of wrapping-up seeds is a very varied one. The way it is done is a clue to how the seeds will be dispersed. Gardeners need to know this information, especially if they intend to try plant breeding because if the seed is not harvested at the right time, nature might well have already taken it elsewhere.

The poppies and bluebells (*Endymion non-scriptus*) use a 'pepper pot' to shake out the seeds whereas broom, sweet pea and *Impatiens* have pods that split so violently that the resulting small explosion throws seeds over a wide area. Berries and others are commonly eaten by a range of animals and the action of the digestive system helps the seeds to germinate when they pass out in their excreta. What is more they have their own fertiliser supply. The fact that seeds are unharmed by this process can be seen in the sludge of any sewage works. Seeds readily germinate, grow and the resulting plants flourish. Tomatoes are particularly good at performing this act.

Many weeds owe part of their success to the efficient way they are dispersed. Dandelion (*Taraxacum officinale*), ragwort (*Senecio jacobaea*), groundsel (*Senecio vulgaris*) and willow herb (*Epilobium* species) all have hairy outgrowths which spread out from the seeds and act like hanggliders when they catch the wind. *Clematis* species use the same method so it is not all bad news if clouds of seeds are seen drifting across the garden.

Some plants have seeds so small, so dust-like, that they need no animal or wind to carry them. Orchids and *Begonia* both fall into this category. In sowing these minute objects it is best to mix them with sharp sand and sow the lot as normal. There is no need to cover them with compost.

A few flowering plants use a spongy layer which traps air. It is used by water lilies (*Nymphaea* species) and alder trees (*Alnus glutinosa*) to enable their seeds to float in the water for a short while and then sink in order to germinate.

Always collect seed when it just reaches ripeness, this will probably mean visiting the plants several times. If time is short, try putting muslin bags over seed heads to catch the seeds as they fall or are thrown. Watch out for the explosive seed pods and capsules as if these are left unenclosed in a dry place indoors they will throw their seed over the whole room.

SEED SOWING

Seeds need at least three requirements: water, warmth and oxygen. Whatever medium the seeds are sown in, be it soil, sterilised compost or totally artificial material, it must have sufficient moisture for germination. Through the same hole that the pollen grain tube entered to fertilise the egg goes the moisture. In the larger seeds this hole can be seen.

Take broad bean seeds for example. If these are soaked in water for a few hours then squeezed, bubbles of water are forced out through this small aperture otherwise known as the micropyle.

Because some seeds have such a water-resistant coat around them it pays to chip a small piece off before sowing. Sweet peas fall into this category but any hard-coated seed can be treated in the same way.

Once the water percolates into the seed it mobilises all the systems and activates chemicals called enzymes. Enzymes speed up all the reactions within living things so germination can occur if only the third requirement is provided – oxygen.

Just as we need oxygen to live, so do plants. Whilst we breathe it in as a part of the air we inhale into our lungs, plants absorb it from the gaps between the soil particles.

Some seeds, like poppies, need light to germinate but the vast majority need darkness. Still, the basic rule of sowing to a maximum depth of two or three times the length of the seed seems to suit most plants.

In spite of taking all precautions, seed germination is still sometimes disappointing. This is largely due to a phenomenon called dormancy, that is, a lengthy period before germination is possible.

Some seeds, from plants as diverse as *Delphinium*, orchid, lily and buttercup, have parts of the seeds which need to mature before germination. Others, like beetroot, have a hormone imbalance which can be corrected by washing them thoroughly.

Many seeds need a period of cold before they will sprout. Trees, including conifers, and shrubs fall into this class. The seeds are best placed in a container filled with sand or a peat and sand mix. This is then placed outside, exposed to the elements, during the winter and normal sowing follows in the spring. This method of breaking seed dormancy is known as stratification.

Some seeds have such thick coats, tree peonies (*Paeonia* species) for example, that they need two winters to make them usable. Those that have fleshy coats, rose hips for example, need to be separated from their coats before sowing. If all this sounds like too much trouble for a small number of seeds try stratifying the seeds in ordinary garden soil but remember to mark the area so that it is not disturbed by mistake in the following months.

The ability of batches of seed to germinate, i.e. their viability, decreases as they age. Parsnip (*Pastinaca sativa*) seed will only store for a year, pea (*Pisum sativum*) lasts two years, tomato lasts three years, radish (*Raphanus sativus*) four years and marrow (*Cucurbita pepo ovifera*) lasts six years. Fortunately, limits are set to determine the minimum germination rate. Whereas carrots and leeks are supposed to show at least a 65 per cent germination rate, peas and broad beans have to reach the more exacting 85 per cent minimum level.

SELECTING A SEEDLING

Not all flowering plants are the same. Even in one batch of seedlings there is often a variety of height, flower colour, leaf pattern and growth habit. A nursery worker would select the features that were of most interest and discard the rest. Obviously this does not happen in nature. Charles Darwin knew that. Darwin (1809-82) is most famous for his theory of evolution which says something to all gardeners about how plants are selected naturally. Any batch of seedlings formed by cross-pollination will show variety; in nature, many more seeds are made than will develop into mature flowering plants. Those that do not perish along the way will be best fitted for the natural environment in which they are sown. The sifting process which allows the growth of best-fitted plants Darwin called Natural Selection.

He did not know at the time, but the variation seen

was mostly due to spontaneous changes to the genetic material within the plants – what are now called mutations. Mutations occur in all living things. They are not predictable but because they occur, because they bring about variety and because Natural Selection acts on them, we see such a wealth of living things.

If the plants and animals selected become so different from one another that they will no longer be able to interbreed, they will be separate species. This is the so-called 'Origin of Species' that Darwin described.

People can speed up the Natural Selection process and often do so in the privacy of their own gardens. Whereas large-flowered plants may have very little survival value in nature and therefore not persist, in the gardener's world they may be grown and multiplied forever.

Seeds are the diminutive 'sleeping beauties' which represent the end product of many millions of years of evolutionary history. Whilst most gardeners are most interested in the mature plants that develop from these packages some would say that plants are just a convenient method of producing more seeds. Charles Darwin would certainly have found some truth in this statement because he understood that real success in life on earth is all about survival and few living things have been more successful than the flowering plants.

We have discovered that all flowers have basically the same structure, the plants that produce them are also based on a similar layout. It is this subject that we will turn to next.

4 Plumbing Problems

LEAF STRUCTURE AND FUNCTION

Some gardeners prefer the foliage to the flowers in plants and they certainly have some power to their argument. Take the house plants for example. Not only can we include the colourful *Coleus* species with their range of reds, yellows and oranges but there is also the very distinctive *Dieffenbachia* too. Named after the German botanist J.F. Dieffenbach, these large foliage plants are variously marked with silver, yellow, green and ivory. An alternative name apparently for this plant is 'dumb-cane' since the crystals found within it can paralyse the vocal chords.

Then there are the dramatic attention-getters with large jade-green leaves. Plants like the India-rubber tree (*Ficus elastica decora* with its broader green leaves. Others of the *Ficus* species have now increased the choice to the gardener. *F. elastica* 'Black Prince' has almost black leaves, *F. elastica tricolor* has foliage of mid-green in the centre with cream margins and *F. elastica doescheri* has leaves mottled with dark green, light green and cream.

Others of the *Ficus* genus are useful too. The pointed leaves and arching branches of the weeping fig *F. benjamina*, wavy broad leaves of the fiddle leaf fig *F. lyrata* and small oval leaves of the mistletoe fig, *F. deltoidea* all add to the variety.

It would be impossible to list here all the attractive foliage plants but mention ought to be made of those that use individual leaf shape and colour, like the Swiss cheese plant (*Monstera deliciosa*) and *Begonia rex*, or overall effect of their foliage like the spider plant (*Chlorophytum comosum* 'Variegatum') and *Asparagus*.

Then there is the luxurious, rampant growth of *Tradescantia* which has almost as many forms as there are letters in the alphabet. There is *T. fluminensis* 'Tricolor' which is striped cream and white and tinted with rose, *T. blossfeldiana* 'Variegata' which is similar to 'Tricolor' but has purple undersides and lastly *T. albovittata* with rich green leaves streaked with silver. Other genera often included in the same group are *Zebrina* and *Callisia* both of which are shaped and patterned like the *Tradescantia*.

The volumes of many horticultural encyclopedias can be filled with references to houseplants cultured purely for their leafy loveliness. There are; *Acalypha*, *Aglaonema*, *Acorus*, *Aspidistra*, *Araucaria* (Monkey Puzzle!), *Aucuba*, *Anthurium*, *Aphelandra* just to list some of these 'A's'.

All these plants, in fact most of the plants that have been successful on earth have leaves. What are they meant to do? All leaves have one major job, to make food for the plant. No matter what colour they may be or how they delight the eye they must be able to capture sunlight and make sugar to survive.

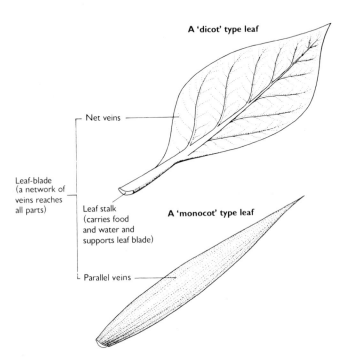

Figure 4.1 The Leaf Story

All leaves are made to the same basic plan. From the outside all leaves are seen to be connected to the main stem by a leaf stalk or petiole (Figure 4.1). Each leaf has a main 'canal system' or midrib running up the centre and if the leaf is flattened – as in most cases – then the surfaces or leaf blades are responsible for food manufacture and riddled with side branches of the midrib.

When a leaf is sliced or snapped in half the real story unfolds. By using a hand-lens or magnifying glass the leaf can be seen as a layered structure. Just like a gateaux, the leaf is divided into regular layers which are amazingly consistent between the thousands of species (Figure 4.2).

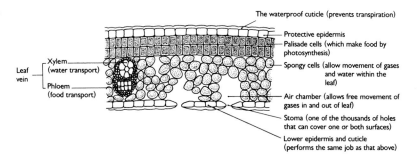

Figure 4.2 The Leaf Revealed

The leaf is a compromise. In order to let the carbon dioxide in to help in sugar-making, the leaf has to put up with losing water at the same time. The lower surface of leaves, and sometimes the upper surface too, is peppered with holes called stomata to allow this exchange to take place.

In daylight the stomata open up. Carbon dioxide gas from the air moves in and water vapour moves out from the leaf to the surrounding air. Although only 0.03 per cent of the atmosphere is made up of carbon dioxide so much is being used by the photosynthesizing leaf that it flows in from the air, a process called diffusion.

From the small spaces on the other side of the stomata the carbon dioxide moves through a watery layer from cell to cell until it finally reaches the palisade cells. This is the type of cell that is responsible for the majority of that miraculous process called photosynthesis.

PHOTOSYNTHESIS

Photosynthesis requires several raw materials to drive it along. It needs sunlight, water, carbon dioxide and chlorophyll (Figure 4.3). The supply of carbon dioxide has been explained, it comes from the air, and sunlight obviously comes from the sun during daylight, but what about the rest?

Chlorophyll is the chemical that makes most plants green. It is found within small structures called chloro-

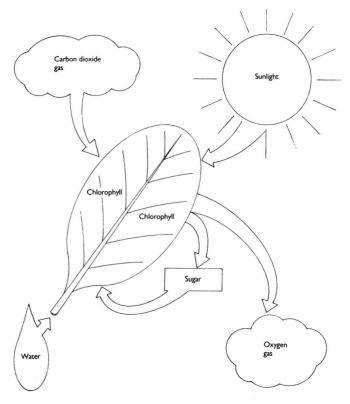

Figure 4.3 Photosynthesis

plasts which are especially numerous within the palisade cells of the leaf. However, any plant cell that contains chlorophyll can carry out photosynthesis. Take the cacti for example.

Cacti are usually leafless, which sounds like a disastrous move; however, since the stem is green this can be used for food production without the dangerous loss of water that leaf possession would involve.

Not all leaves are green of course and the reason for this is not to please the horticulturalist although many have been later bred just for their many-hued foliage, but to assist in filtering light. Interestingly there is not just one type of chlorophyll but a whole series of pigments, the two most common being: chlorophyll a which is blue-green, chlorophyll b which is yellow-green, yellow xanthophyll and orange carotene (the chemical that turns carrot roots orange).

All plants that photosynthesise use chlorophyll a. It can absorb blue and red light particularly well which is fine for those leaves exposed to full sunlight but what about those plants which are naturally found underneath the trees in shady conditions? The filtered light inside woods is not only dimmer – there is less of it – but it has a different make-up too.

What woodland and forest plants need is a selection of pigments able to absorb this filtered light and pass the energy on to chlorophyll a. So chlorophyll b absorbs blue-green light, xanthophyll the greenish-blue light and carotene the blue-violet light. It is these 'chemical assistants' of photosynthesis that we gardeners enjoy looking at so much.

Life in the sun is not all good news though. You can have too much of a good thing. Some plants have discarded some chlorophyll in order to become white in patches to reflect the sun. *Chlorophytum* is an obvious example. The chlorophyll gives the leaf green stripes made for food production and the creamy stripes in between make sure the leaf does not overheat. Sunstroke can be a problem for plants as well as people! Some – plants not people – turn their leaves sideways on to the sun in order to prevent overheating. Apparently, ephemerals make the most of sunlight during their short lives by turning themselves towards the sun; a dangerous strategy in hot, dry places but it pays off.

Many plants that have to persevere in dry, sometimes hot, places have developed a thicker than usual waxy layer or cuticle on their leaves. They are easily picked out because the cuticle is glossy. Most of the so-called foliage plants have this thick cuticle, *Ficus* species for example, which indicates that in the wind they would be found in the top layer of woods and forests where the sunshine and wind speeds are the greatest.

Apart from sunlight, carbon dioxide from the air and chlorophyll within the plant cells, water is needed too. This comes from the soil and has to make the tortuous journey into, across and up the plant before it can be used.

Then, when the conditions are right the most breath-taking process on earth takes place. The water is split asunder by the light and a most valuable waste product is made: oxygen. The gas that we, and all life on earth rely on, is produced as a waste product. In return the carbon dioxide that we produce and breathe out can then be recycled by photosynthesising plants. Clearly people and plants are interdependent, we depend on each other for survival.

When light breaks down water, hydrogen is also made and when this combines with carbon dioxide taken from the air, glucose sugar is formed and some water too. This sugar is the raw material of life. From it every other material can be made, not only new plant parts but new animal parts too, because plants are the basic food for all animals.

Have you talked to your plants lately? You should because if they have enough sunlight, the next factor that will make them grow is extra carbon dioxide and, yes, you have guessed it, by breathing all over them you will provide free carbon dioxide and plenty of it. Of course professional growers do not go and 'chat up' their vast numbers of plants, instead they enrich the carbon dioxide content of the air with gas burners.

After increasing the amount of carbon dioxide the next step is to increase the temperature. Do not think that if you cannot increase the carbon dioxide then a temperature increase will do instead. It has to be in the order: extra light, then carbon dioxide, then temperature.

Leaves not only are the 'factories' for producing food but can also act as the 'warehouses' that store it. Bulbs are composed of fleshy leaves that contain stored food. All the daffodils, tulips and onions rely on this means of energy store so that the excess of food production in the summer can be used the following spring for a quick 'getaway'.

TRANSPIRATION

Stephen Hales was born in 1677 into a prominent Kent family. Later he was to enter Cambridge University and after that became Vicar at Teddington where he was so strict that any sinners had to do public penance.

However, it is Hales' work with plants and animals that was published in his book *Vegetable Staticks* in 1727 that made him famous. For example, he reported that a sunflower (*Helianthus annuus*) over a yard (1 m) high lost 1 lb 14 oz (0.9 kg) of water in twelve hours. The same plant was found to have a surface area of 39 sq ft (3.6 sq m). This is a remarkable figure when compared with the surface area of the human body which, according to Hales, is about 15 sq ft (1.4 sq m).

Although Hales referred to this water-loss as 'perspiration' today we use the term transpiration, and Hales' findings have been confirmed by those made more recently. Large trees like oaks and beeches are known to lose up to 100 gallons (455 litres) on a summer's day through transpiration.

STEMS – THE SUPPORT SYSTEM

Hales' experiments with vines proved the value of stems too. He watched vine stems push their sap up to 25 ft (7.6 m) in a single day. Later he cut into the side of an oak branch and on the opposite side, at a different height, he repeated the process. In spite of such brutality the branch continued to lose water by transpiration. So stems must act as a pipeline for water between the roots and leaves.

Another job that stems must do is to hold the leaves in the best place to capture sunlight so that food can be made during photosynthesis. Also stems hold flowers in the best place for pollination; flowers need to show their wares and stems make sure they do just that.

Stems can be used for food storage too. The tips of underground stems can become swollen as in the potato and artichoke. Technically these are known as stem tubers. Other underground stems become swollen with food reserves along their whole length. Iris, Solomon's seal (*Polygonatum*) and that dastardly couch grass (*Agropyron repens*) all use this method known as a rhizome. The familiar *Gladiolus* and *Crocus* corms are in fact short, vertical underground stems swollen with food reserves.

Underground side branches can turn up, produce buds and grow out of the soil to develop into new plants. Mint (*Mentha*) and pear trees both grow in this way. If the side branches grow along the ground and root at intervals separate plants develop as in strawberry and the weeds like creeping buttercup. If a weak stem, rather than a side branch, touches the ground, roots and then sends off a side branch then it is described as a stolon. Blackberries use this method.

Stems also make extra food. Whenever they are green they photosynthesise and every little helps in nature. It also means that they will grow faster which is good news for the gardener.

Inside the stem it is 'all systems go' and there is no room for inefficiency. Around the outside of green stems there is a waterproof layer just as in the leaf (Figure 4.4). Inside that are cells which support the rest of the tissue as well as store food and often can make it too.

The rest of the stem consists of transport cells. There are xylem cells which help water move up from the root to the leaves, phloem cells which move food up and down the plant and in between are cambium cells which make either xylem or phloem as they multiply.

Two botanists by the name of Dixon and Joly first put

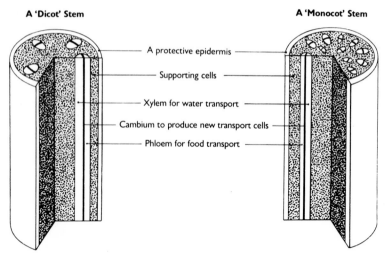

Figure 4.4 The Stem Story

forward the theory which helps explain how water reaches the leaves even in the tallest of trees. They argued that as water has such a liking for its own company, or cohesion, whenever it is lost from leaves it will drag more of itself into the leaf. In the same way a column of water will be pulled up the stem from the root. Though it might look calm enough outside, inside the stem is a cauldron of activity with materials moving through it in all directions all the time.

Fruit trees can be encouraged to fruit by 'ringing' the tree. This is a method of cutting down the downward flow of foods and hormones by using one of several methods. Most severely a narrow ring of bark can be taken out right to the heartwood (see Figure 4.5) about 2 ft (60 cm) above soil level. In order that this can heal over in the summer it needs to be done in late April.

Less dramatic is the taking out of two semicircular rings on opposite sides of the trunk a few inches (cm) apart. If individual branches are not fruiting a sharp knife could be drawn around the branch or a thin wire twisted around it early in the spring. Again this must be done early enough to allow recovery and if wire is used it should be removed during the summer.

ROOTS – THE ANCHORAGE SYSTEM

At the base of the plant are roots. Though they may take all shapes and forms all roots perform the same basic four jobs. First, they have to anchor the plant to the ground.

Though it might seem like common sense not to allow geraniums and roses to be blown about the garden it is vital to their lives that they remain in one place.

After all, green plants need to obtain water for photosynthesis as well as mineral salts. The roots absorb water from the soil which has particles of plant food dissolved in it. The next job of roots is to act as a pipeline between the soil and stem.

To do these jobs properly roots have one of two main designs. Some plants use a very large main root called a tap root. There are usually numerous small roots penetrating from the tap root and this system is used by carrots, and by weeds like dandelion.

The alternative strategy is to have a mass of narrow adventitious roots which develop directly from the base of the stem. Many ephemerals and annuals use this rooting method along with the more familiar grasses.

Roots can become adapted to other functions. Food storage is of prime importance in biennials. These plants grow and then store in the first growing season. During the second season this food is used to enable the plant to flower and produce seed. Carrots fall into this category and they are picked at the end of the first season so that the tap roots are swollen with food. Dahlias use swollen fibrous roots to store food too.

When Is A Root A Stem?

It seems unlikely, if not downright awkward, to have stems found beneath the soil where the roots should be or roots in the air where shoots are usually expected. Take the potato tuber which is the tip of the stem yet is found under the soil or the Swiss cheese plant aerial roots often found dangling great distances above the compost.

How can you tell the difference between stems and roots? In the germinating seed the root always appears first and turns downwards. The stem appears next and always turns upwards. Stems often bear leaves and buds but roots bear a weft of tiny, water-absorbing root hairs.

Because the points where leaves appear are called nodes then these can be used to identify stems. Roots never have nodes and consequently lack the spaces between nodes, or internodes, as they are known. Certainly stems are green whereas roots are usually a brown or cream colour.

To protect them as they push through the soil, roots have developed a protective lid or root cap at their tips.

This is seen very easily in aerial roots, as in the Swiss cheese plant.

The final and irrevocable step is to cut through the unknown structure and use a magnifying glass or hand lens to inspect the internal structure. Stems have transport systems which are situated away from the central position. Roots, on the other hand, have the transport gathered together as a central core which runs up the centre like a single strand.

HORMONES

The familiar pathway from birth through puberty to adulthood in humans is made possible by the action of chemicals called hormones. Hormones are also to be found in plants where they also control growth and development including flowering.

In 1881 Charles Darwin published a paper called 'The Power of Movement in Plants'. He had found that by covering the very tip of seedlings, with opaque glass caps, they did not curve towards light like normal seedlings. Furthermore, he found that although light was detected by the plant tip it was the area immediately below it that responded. Today we know that hormones called auxins are made by the tip and transported down the stem where they make the plant cells expand.

The full story has not yet been revealed but it is clear that the plant cells expand most where the auxin hormones are concentrated. Leaves and sometimes whole plants lean towards light because auxin is produced by the shoot tip and transported mostly to the shady side of the plant. The result is that the shady side expands more than the sunny side and the plant grows towards the light. Root tips produce auxins too but in smaller quantities and here they control growth towards water and away from light.

It is an often noted fact that as the main shoot grows upwards the side shoots are not allowed to develop. It is auxins that make this possible by diverting water and food to the tip and away from the side or lateral buds. During normal plant development this may persist so that one main shoot remains, as in the Scots pine, otherwise during ageing the side shoots grow and a rounded rather than pointed plant grows, like an ash tree for example.

Gardeners can use this knowledge to their advantage. By taking off the stem tip the plant should develop its side shoots and become bushy. Hedges grow more dense because they are regularly trimmed and flowering pot plants are made more floriferous if the growing tips are pinched out early in life.

These days laboratories make artificial or synthetic auxins which are used in hormone rooting to stimulate root production in cuttings, help fruit to be produced even when pollination has not occurred – as in seedless grapes, prevent hedges and grass growing too fast when sprayed on to them and also interfere with plant growth so much that they can be used for selective weed-killers.

In rooting powder a synthetic auxin by the name of 2, 4–dichlorophenoxyacetic acid, otherwise known as 2,4-D, is mixed with an inert powder. When added to the base of cuttings new roots grow which are often described as adventitious because they are not true roots but will still do the job of water absorption. Fruit growers who need to be certain of a good crop can spray 2,4-D on to the flowers and fruit 'set' follows.

Whilst high doses of 2,4-D slow down the growth of leaves in hedges and lawns, when very high concentrations are used plants suffer. This fact can be used to kill plants when necessary because broad-leaved weeds in the lawn absorb more than the grasses. So when 2,4-D is sprayed on to them the weeds become distorted and eventually wither leaving a first-class turf.

In the 1920s Japanese farmers found some rice seedlings grew much taller than normal. Later it was discovered that these plants were infected with a fungus that made hormones called gibberellins. It was the gibberellins that made the internodes grow.

Earlier the work of the geneticist Gregor Mendel was explained. He had worked with tall and dwarf pea plants. We know today that the tall plants have genes which instruct them to make the full amount of gibberellins whereas dwarf plants have genes which tell them to make only a small amount and so they cannot grow as tall. In laboratories gibberellins have been added to dwarf plants and they have grown to a normal size.

Chrysanthemums can be tall or dwarf for the same reason and if they are tall a dose of 2,4-D in their compost can inhibit their growth so that they do not grow too tall. If they are later removed from their pots to the garden they soon go back to their normal tall habit.

In 1956 the Kinin hormones were discovered. These were found to bring about cell division in plants when auxins are present and have been used extensively in laboratories to try to make whole plants from single cells.

Another hormone by the name of abscisin is responsible for 'shutting down' the plant factory when winter
arrives. In deciduous trees and shrubs it is involved in
separating the leaves from the plant so that less water is
lost during the coldest months. Dying leaves are also
pumped full of waste products, which often help give
them their autumn colours, and are then shed.

FLOWERING TIME

A chemical by the name of phytochrome is found in all
flowering plants, in two interconvertible forms. During
daylight a form called P725 is made which is active but
during the night another, inactive, form called P665 is
made.

Stems elongate in the dark and not in the day so plants
will grow taller at night. On the other hand leaves
expand during daylight and not at night. Side roots grow
best in darkness and are slowed down by light. Lastly,
flowers develop depending on alternating periods of light
and dark.

Basically there are three groups of flowers. Some need
long days, about 10 hours minimum, and short nights
and are called long-day plants. They include lettuce,
spinach, carnations, radishes and petunias.

As expected there are also short-day plants that require
short days and long nights. These include poinsettias and
Chrysanthemums. Of course if gardeners need plants
flowering out of season they can alter the day length
artifically. The length of daylight needed to induce
flowering in short-day and long-day plants varies. For
example, *Chrysanthemum* can be given less than $9\frac{1}{2}$ hours
daylight and they will develop flower buds. Long-day
plants like carnations will need to be given artificial light
to lengthen the day if early flowering is required out of
season.

The same phytochrome chemical is used here but long-
day plants need great amounts of P725, made during
sunlight, whereas short-day plants need an accumulation
of P665, made at night. It must be said that some plants,
like tomato and cotton, are called day-neutral because
they are indifferent to day-length.

All flowers are thought to use a hormone called
'florigen' which has not yet been isolated but is thought
to be formed after phytochrome has been affected by
day-length. Eventually, someone will find out whether it
is a single substance or a series of substances that bring
about that most important event, flowering.

BARK

Since trees and shrubs grow to such heights they need extra support and supplies of water which are not demanded by annuals or biennials. To do this they become woody as opposed to the herbaceous, or non-woody, plants which die down with frosts.

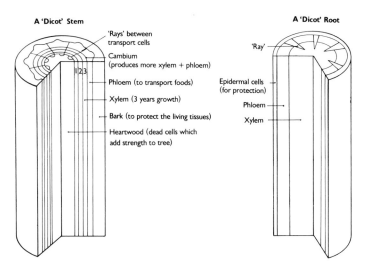

Figure 4.5 What Happens When Plants Go Woody

It is the cambium tissue (Figure 4.5) that makes wood growth possible in roots and stems. Whilst it is initially limited to small groups of cells inside each group of transport cells they divide to link together to form a ring. As soon as this is completed water-conducting xylem cells are made to the inside and food-transporting cells to the outside. In the stems columns of ordinary plant cells strike out between the transport tissues so that sideways, as well as vertical, movement of materials can take place.

Much more xylem is made than phloem with the result that eventually the bulk of the stem and root is occupied by xylem – the wood. This type of growth is made during the middle months of the year. In the spring the first-formed xylem consists of large vessels. As the year progresses the xylem cells get gradually smaller and the wood is denser. The result is that a series of concentric annual rings are made each of which are composed of one season's growth. Each ring tells the tale of one year in the life of that plant so not only can the age of trees be estimated accurately by counting the rings but the weather in that year can be described too. Cold, dry springs lead to formation of smaller xylem in smaller numbers than usual and warm, wet summers produce many xylem cells which are larger than usual.

In order that the surface of the stem does not crack and burst open with all this growth there is a special process which occurs near the surface and makes the familiar corky bark. This protective layer is sometimes split into scales as in the plane (*Platanus*) or pine (*Pinus*) trees. Bark can be just $\frac{1}{16}$ in (2 mm) thick, as in cherries, or up to 1 ft (30 cm) deep, as in the cork oak (*Quercus suber*) or giant redwoods. It is so vital that if animals like deer and rabbits remove a complete ring around the trunk not only can infections enter the tree but transport to and from the roots is halted and the plant frequently dies.

Some trees and shrubs are grown purely for the treat of seeing their bark. There are birches (*Betula* species), dogwoods (*Cornus* species), willows (*Salix* species), maples (*Acer* species) and some even 'peel off' their bark, as does the paperbark maple (*Acer griseum*), or even show different colours as they do so, as does the 'snake-bark' maple (*Acer pensylvanicum*).

Wine from Trees
Some gardeners, not being content with just looking at their trees, like to use them for wine-making. Sugar maple (*Acer saccharum*) is well known for its contribution to sugar maple syrup but silver birch (*Betula pendula*), walnut (*Juglans regia*) and sycamore (*Acer pseudoplatanus*) can be used too.

During late March and early April when the buds burst into green growth a hole can be drilled into the trunk, sloping slightly upwards. The hole needs to be only 1 in (2 cm) across and deep and this can be plugged with a cork fitted with one end of a piece of plastic tubing. The other end of the tube is best placed into a clean plastic container which is sealed to prevent insects and other pests entering. After one gallon (4.5 litres) of sap is collected seal the hole in the tree with a solid cork and proprietary sealant. This process can be repeated the following season. The sap should be boiled to kill any bacterial infection and then it can replace water in any wine recipe. It imparts a very distinctive bouquet and flavour to the wine.

Whatever the reason gardeners put plants in their gardens, be it for their flowers, foliage, bark or maybe even their sap, they will not achieve their best unless given the correct soil conditions. It is to this topic that we will turn next.

5 Can You Dig It?

SOIL STRUCTURE AND TEXTURE

No matter whether your plot consists of a large estate, a small town garden or just a window-box, the plants that grow in it are greatly influenced by the type of soil they grow in.

Soil is a mixture of four main ingredients: rock, water, air and organic matter. The vast variety of soil types that can be seen across the world are just different mixtures of this basic recipe.

Rock particles make up about 45 per cent of most soils. Where soils are just being formed naturally they can be all rock but with peaty soils the opposite is true and these may have little or no rock at all. Eventually the large boulders are broken into smaller ones and mineral particles are formed which can be of various sizes (Figure 5.1).

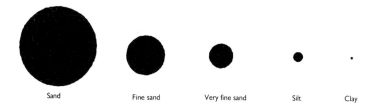

Figure 5.1 Sand, Silt and Clay Particles

Any particle less than 2 mm but more than 0.05 mm diameter is known as sand. The virtue of sandy soils is that they contain a lot of air between their particles which warms up quickly in the spring – or in a propagator for that matter – and so can germinate seeds quickly in the first part of the growing season. Sandy soils are easily worked when wet.

The network of fine channels in the soil also means that it will drain quickly. This property is a mixed blessing since rapid drainage is ideal in periods of heavy rainfall but can be disastrous in drought conditions. Also many plant foods are dissolved in the water passing through the sandy soil and are lost in drainage water. This process is often called leaching and soils with a high proportion of sand in them are often very short of plant nutrients and nicknamed 'hungry' because of this.

At the other end of the rock particles scale comes the clay. Clay particles are always less than 0.002 mm diameter. The great advantage with clay is that it possesses certain electrical charges which attract plant foods, in fact most nutrients are associated with clay particles.

However, pure clay soils – or those with a high clay content – are often waterlogged. The water drains very slowly through the fine channels between the particles. What is more, because the clay soil pores are often water filled they are very slow to warm up in the spring and so not suitable for early crops. Also they are very heavy to work – 'backbreaking' – because of their water content and their ability to stick together.

In the summer clay soils often shrink, then swell when waterlogged, and wide cracks can appear which is yet another problem for the would-be gardener. The surface may become so hard during droughts that this soil is almost unworkable.

Silt soil particles are between 0.05 and 0.002 mm in diameter and show intermediate properties to clays and sands. They are not ideal soils, though, because they lack sufficient organic matter. Frequently they become cloddy and preparation of a good seed bed is very difficult. A heavy downpour of rain causes a cap of silt particles to form on the soil surface preventing the sprouting of seeds.

How can gardeners tell what kind of soil they have? Simple, try the 'Hillman handful' test. Choose a day when the soil is moist and carefully expose the top spit – one spade depth – with a spade or trowel. Examine the soil carefully (Figure 5.2).

Is it full of stones spread throughout the soil? If so you have – you have guessed it – stony soil. This is generally free draining and easily worked in the spring but dries out quickly in the summer and is difficult to cultivate. On the other hand is the soil very dark in colour and very spongy to the feel? If so, this is a peaty soil. This is easy to work and very fertile if limed and drained. Unfortunately it is often too acid for most plants, before it is treated. Many gardeners tolerate a shallow dark soil with whitish soil beneath. This is a limy or chalky soil which is ideally suited to rockery plants but soft and sticky in wet weather.

Other soils are best felt rather than just looked at. Pick up a generous handful of the soil and carefully mould it

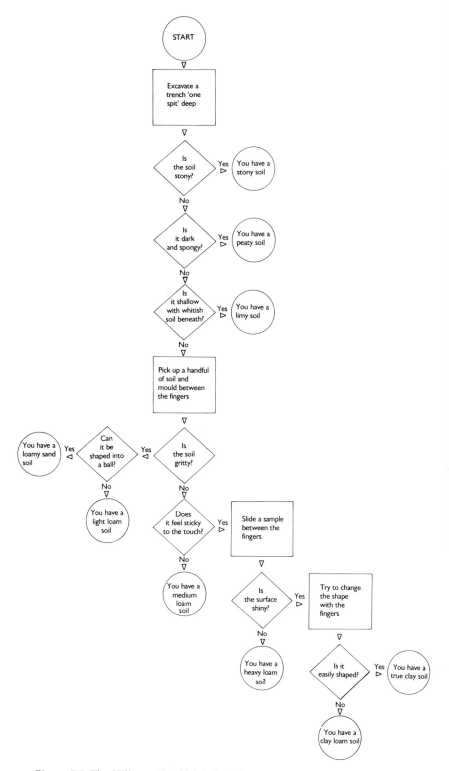

Figure 5.2 The Hillman Handful Soil Test

between the fingers. If it is gritty – geologists test this by grinding it between their teeth, but this is not advisable – and can be shaped into a ball without crumbling it can be called a loamy sand. If it is very similar but does crumble then it is best described as a light loam. Both loamy sands and light loams are easily warmed by the spring weather and are suitable for early crops. They are easily worked even when wet because they are so free draining. However, they lose plant foods in their drainage water and so need heavy applications of fertilisers. Also they dry out quickly and need frequent watering during drought conditions.

On the other hand, if the handful of soil is not gritty and does not feel sticky it is a medium loam. If the sample is sticky try sliding a sample between the thumb and fingers. If the surface does not become shiny you have a heavy loam and if it is try to change the shape of the soil with your fingers. With clay loams the shape can only be changed with difficulty whereas with true clays the soil can be easily shaped. Though soils with clays are well supplied with plant foods they are, as mentioned earlier, so slow to warm up in the spring that they are not suitable for early crops. Any gardener who has clay soil in their garden knows what backache can be caused by trying to work this soil in wet conditions. It tends to waterlog quickly and cracks and cakes hard during the summer months.

SOIL IS A LIVING THING

The few gardeners that possess loam for a garden soil are amongst the most fortunate people in the world. Not only does a loam possess the correct proportions of sand, silt and clay but also it will have the correct amounts of water, air and organic material.

The sand and silt ensure that there are some large spaces between some of the soil particles. During normal conditions these spaces will be largely air-filled and in wet weather the spaces will allow enough drainage to prevent waterlogging. Plant roots, just like stems and leaves, need air – and in particular the oxygen within it – and when water enters soils it is vital air that is forced out.

On the other hand, water is also needed by roots and it is the clay particles that take hold of the water and all the plant foods inside it. Soils are living things. Under natural, uncultivated conditions all the dead plant and animal materials are quickly broken down by earthworms, insects, fungi and bacteria until they no longer resemble their original condition and form a substance well known to gardeners, humus. Humus is normally a brown, spongy material found on the surface of soils.

Because bacteria are microscopic, the largest are only 0.0002 in (0.005 mm) in length, they are so easily overlooked by the gardener and yet so abundant and vital that further examination is necessary. Bacteria are simple, single-celled plants that are as small as clay particles.

They multiply so rapidly, dividing once every 20 minutes or so, that under ideal conditions a single bacterium could divide over a 24-hour period to produce 17,000,000 offspring. If this continued over a six-day period their bulk would be enough to fill a sphere the size of the earth. Fortunately the ideal warmth, water, oxygen, food and space are not available otherwise we should need to spend more time scraping bacteria off the garden than cultivating it.

Bacteria are in their greatest numbers near the surface of the soil where more ideal conditions are to be found. In every ounce of soil there are up to 84,000,000,000 bacteria (3,400,000,000 per gram). In the top 6 in (15 cm) of each acre (0.4 ha) of fertile soil there are about 2,860 lb (1,300 kg) of bacteria. Their numbers vary considerably during the year and so, as one might expect, when conditions are warm and wet they are very numerous when compared with the colder depths of winter.

Whenever organic – living – matter falls on the soil, be it leaves, petals or dead animals, the bacteria invade and decompose it until they can obtain no further nourishment from it. They usually hand over to the fungi, the next in a line of garbage-disposal experts.

So far over 700 species of fungi have been found living within the soil. Since fungi are not green, and therefore cannot make their own food using light like most plants, they have to seek out their food. The broken down products of bacterial action are an ideal source of nutrition for fungi.

Whilst most people think of toadstools and mushrooms when fungi are mentioned, these are just one group. Other groups are yeasts and moulds. Again, most people think of beer and wine-making when yeasts are mentioned but the soil is brimming with them.

Moulds are the most important fungi as far as gardeners are concerned. There are about 570 million of these in every ounce of fertile soil (20 million per gram) and in terms of weight there are up to a ton per top six ins per acre of soil (2,500 kg per 15 cm per ha). When the moulds have done their job it is the turn of animals, such as the earthworms.

Imagine sitting in a jungle by night, it would be cool, dark and steam-filled. Now you have an idea of what it must be like to live in the soil, a place where earthworms feel very much at home.

There are many species of earthworms, they vary in size from $\frac{1}{2}$ in (1 cm) to a 'wonderworm' reported in 1937 which was found in South Africa and said to be 22 ft (6.7 m) long when naturally extended.

As earthworms tunnel through soil they swallow, then grind the soil in their stomachs. Digestive juices are poured on to the food releasing many plant nutrients which are pushed out of the worm along with other waste products. If this excreta is deposited on the soil surface worm 'casts' are said to have been made. Every year up to a staggering 16,000 lb per acre (20,000 kg per ha) of worm casts can be manufactured.

Worms are no sluggards. Up to 15 tons of soil per acre (37,500 kg per ha) can pass through earthworms every year. It is believed by ardent worm watchers – the spirit of Gilbert White is not dead – that every 60 to 70 years the top 6 in (15 cm) of soil is passed through worms.

As well as increasing the plant food content of soils worms also produce holes for drainage and aeration, recycle the earth by moving the lower soil to the surface and also drag humus down into the soil.

Earthworms are found in the highest numbers, up to 3,000,000 per acre (7,500,000 per ha) in moist, well-drained and aerated soils which are also high in lime. Any generous application of farmyard manure (known in polite circles as FYM) will help to increase worm numbers. You could have up to 15 cwt of wriggling 'worm power' per acre (2,000 kg per ha).

IMPROVING YOUR SOIL

There are few gardeners who can profess to having a loam for their soil. Loams are so perfectly balanced that they hold on to just enough water, food and air to support healthy plant growth. By using occasional applications of fertilisers, lime and humus-making matter the loams will stay in perfect trim.

But what about the others, the majority, you cry? Well, stony soils must have the largest stones removed but not all the stones. Many an over-enthusiastic novice has sieved the whole of their garden soil only to find that the soil collapsed and would not allow proper plant growth any longer. Because drainage water leaches out the plant foods from stony soils these must be replenished using fertilisers. Application of humus will enable the soil to hold on to more water and foods. Never dig or apply treatments too deeply or they will be quickly washed away.

Peat-rich soils are another story. They are very fertile but can be waterlogged and very acidic. If they are well-drained by adding sand or land-drains and made less acidic by adding lime the peats can prove a winner every time.

Chalk-rich soils can be greatly improved too. Because they are generally shallow, digging should not be deep and their fast drainage should be slowed down by adding humus perhaps in the form of manure. Since they are free-draining, fertilisers are a 'must' too.

Sands (the 'hungry soils') are so free-draining that they are the worst soil type in terms of losing water and foods. Although adding fertilisers will be a good short-term policy they will usually be lost that season so food-retentive humus must be incorporated into the surface layers too.

Last are the clay-rich soils. Unlike sandy soils these are very heavy and difficult to work. Because they drain very slowly, in the final resort gardeners might need to use heavy duty land drains to solve the problem – an expensive solution.

Still the heavy work is not over. The weather is a free agent that can be used to help break up clayey soils but first the gardener must dig the plot over roughly each autumn so that the large pieces of clay are exposed to the winter frosts that will shatter them. Once again lime can be used, but this time it is not to counteract acidity but help the clay particles accumulate with the humus and each other in a process that goes by the grand name of flocculation (figure 5.3).

When flocculation occurs small 'crumbs' of soil are made which consist of sand, silt, clay and humus. The soil is said to have a good crumb structure – a 'fine tilth' – if all the large clods have been broken down so that the whole area consists of small soil crumbs. Such a fine soil is best for all plant growth, from germinating seeds to mature plants. In this condition the soil should crumble easily between the fingers and is known as 'friable'.

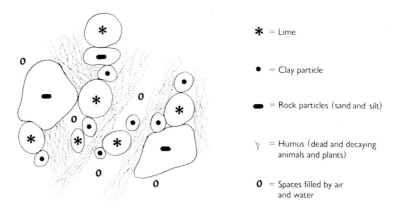

Figure 5.3 *Flocculation of Clay in Soils*

WHAT DOES 'pH' MEAN?

'pH' is one of the most revered abbreviations used in gardening. Why should this be? Well, it stands for the jargon 'hydrogen ion concentration'. If that is very little help, and there is little reason why it should be, read on.

Most people have tasted lemon juice and vinegar – though probably not at the same time – and these are both acids. All acids have the same sour taste. Bicarbonate of soda, which might be taken to relieve indigestion, is an alkaline substance. Sometimes alkalis are described as sweet but this is probably more due to their being opposite to acids than any real sweet taste.

Soils can be sour and sweet too. Some gardeners from previous generations used to taste their soil to see if it was sour, and acid, or sweet, and alkaline, but due to all the 'wee beasties' in it this is not a recommended practice.

How do soils become sour or sweet? Water is composed of two electrically charged parts, or ions, one of which is hydrogen on its own and the other is hydrogen attached to oxygen. It is the hydrogen ions that effect the soil pH.

When water drains through soil the hydrogen ions replace plant foods attached to the clay particles and if this leaching process continues for too long, the hydrogen ions build up so much that the soil become acidic. So acidic soils have lost most of their plant foods.

Alkaline soils do not have many hydrogen ions but they do have vast supplies of calcium ions instead. Limestones and chalk bedrocks are the most common source of calcium ions but they can be added artificially by applications of lime. Unfortunately, very alkaline soils have few nutrients that are available to plants. Calcium 'locks up' the foods.

As you might gather, very acidic and very alkaline soils are bad news for gardeners. What is needed is a soil which lies between the two, in other words a neutral soil.

The fertility of a soil can be easily gauged by finding out its pH. The pH scale runs from 1 to 14 where 1 is the most acidic, 14 is the most alkaline and 7 is neutral.

For each pH unit change there is a tenfold difference in hydrogen ion concentration. This means that a pH 3 soil is ten times more concentrated than a pH 4 soil so although both are acidic the first soil is ten times more acidic. Soils usually range from pH 3 for the most acidic and pH 10.5 for the most alkaline. However, the normal range for humid areas is from 5 to 7.5 and for dry, arid areas it is more like 6.5 to 9. A very wide range of garden plants will flourish when the pH is between 6.5 and 7.

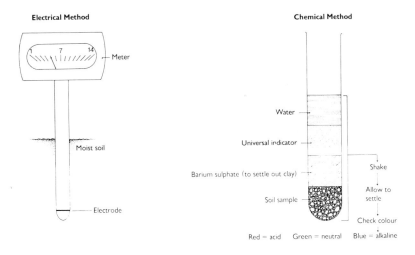

Figure 5.4 Do It Yourself Soil pH Test

These days it is possible for amateur gardeners to test their soils for pH. There are basically two types of pH test, electrical and chemical. Electrical tests work by a metal probe being placed in the soil (Figure 5.4). The hydrogen ions are detected by the probe and a readout gives the pH. The soil needs to be just moist enough to make this test work properly.

Chemical pH tests usually involve filling a tube with small, equal amounts of soil, barium sulphate, universal indicator solution and water (Figure 5.4). The whole tube is sealed and the contents mixed. Universal indicator changes colour depending on the pH of the soil – red for acidic, green for neutral and blue for alkaline – and barium sulphate makes the clay particles flocculate and settle out quickly. After ten minutes the colour can be compared with a chart and the pH determined.

The pH of soils, potting mixtures, fertilisers and even water used for plants are all important. Only a comparatively few plants can tolerate really acidic soil. There are *Rhododendron*, *Camellia*, most *Ericas* and many tropical plants which can put up with these conditions and their old collective name was the 'calcifuges'. They make good 'indicator plants' because whenever you see a calcifuge you will know the soil is acidic.

Other plants tolerate alkaline soils better. They used to be called 'calcicoles' and, as might be expected, include many alpines from the limestone and chalk areas of the world. The cabbage family (*Cruciferae*) belong in this group too and it is as well to remember that these include wallflower (*Cheiranthus*) as well as the familiar cabbages, Brussels sprouts and turnips. Once again, these indicator plants are useful in guessing the pH of a soil without actually testing it.

In acid soils dressings of lime will help to neutralise the acidity but since acidity is often due to bad drainage regular cultivation can help too. Alkaline soils can be made more acid by adding substances like *Sphagnum* peat and leafmould, especially from oak, or chemicals. Any sulphate fertiliser can be used too, like ammonium or iron or aluminium sulphate, because when these dissolve in water very dilute sulphuric acid is made. Some gardeners use a pure bed of peat raised above the normal garden level to cultivate their calcifuges. It is best to have at least 2 ft (60 cm) depth of material in a raised peat bed but if deeply rooting plants are used a greater depth will need to be considered. Peat beds last longer if they are raised rather than sunk into the normal garden level.

COMPOSTS AND MIXES

Whether you are a British gardener using composts or an American one using mixes (or mixtures), you are using the same material whether it be for germinating seeds or growing on mature plants. Garden soil is very unsuitable for this because of all the harmful living things to be found within it, even earthworms are not wanted inside pots and other containers.

As far as soil-based composts are concerned the John

Innes Horticultural Institute have set the standard by devising ideal mixtures. There are three basic JI recipes, for seed, cutting and potting composts, and all of them are based on volume. Seed mixtures are composed of 2 parts loam, 1 part peat and 1 part coarse sand. To each bushel (0.036 m^3) 1½ oz (45 g) of superphosphate of lime and ¾ oz (20 g) of finely ground chalk or limestone should be added. The cuttings mixture is very simple and composed of 1 part loam, 2 parts peat and 1 part coarse sand.

Potting mixtures vary depending on their use. Basically they are all 7 parts loam, 3 parts peat and 2 parts coarse sand. JI potting compost No. 1 has ¾ oz (20 g) of ground chalk or limestone, 4 oz (110 g) of a mixture of 2 parts (by weight) hoof and horn meal, 2 parts superphosphate of lime and 1 part of sulphate of potash.

Plants in pots greater than 4 in (10 cm) diameter have double the chalk and fertiliser mixture and this is known as JI potting compost No. 2. For any plants in pots of 8 in (20 cm) diameter or more the chalk and fertiliser additives are tripled. Although John Innes mixtures are not readily available in the USA, they can be made up according to the above recipes.

These mixtures represent the best deal that plants can get from soil. Unfortunately all these standard mixtures are alkaline because of the chalk or limestone added so if any lime-hating calcifuge plants are grown sulphur dust, known as flowers of sulphur, replaces the chalk or limestone.

Soil varies such a lot that composts based on peat have been devised with the addition of sand, vermiculite (a light flake made from heating minerals), perlite (an air-filled granule made by heating volcanic rock), polystyrene chips and fertilisers plus limestone to make the compost pH about neutral. In the United States of America, Cornell University did much of the early work on peat-based mixtures, so much so that they are often referred to as Cornell mixes.

Since the plant foods are limited in peat-based composts fertilisers must be added after a couple of months. Occasionally slow-release fertilisers are added, as in grow bags (peat modules), so that crops like tomatoes can be grown throughout the season without any additions of fertilisers. Grow bags have made the cultivation of plants on as small an area as a balcony possible as well as having a range of uses apart from tomato cultivation, including rooting cuttings and germinating seeds.

THE GREAT DEBATE – SOIL OR PEAT-BASED MIXTURES?

The arguments over whether soil or peat-based mixtures are best continues. Soilless composts are lighter than soil in weight. This means that although they may be easier to transport when dry the plants growing in them can also be unstable and easily dislodged. When placing plants in peat they do not need to be firmed in so well but there is a much greater chance of drying out. As mentioned previously, peat is inherently infertile so soil comes out better here. In the end perhaps the argument is misdirected and really gardeners ought to concern themselves more with using their mixtures correctly rather than worrying over whether their neighbour has a better mix.

All good growing mixtures are sterilised. This means that all life within the compost has been done away with by means of chemicals or heat. This means that at the beginning the only form of life in the pot is the plant, but many forms of life, including bacteria and fungi, will soon invade it. The idea is that the plant gets a 'flying start' in a perfect mixture of water, air and fertilisers before there is competition from any other living thing.

Over long periods plant roots will take nutrients from their growing mixture and in return give hydrogen ions back. This means that over a period of time the roots make the mixture more acidic or 'sour'. The only solution here is to repot the plant in a fresh mixture.

Garden soil is so important to plants, that every effort must be taken to keep it in 'tiptop' condition. The application of garden compost and manure are very important in this respect and it is to these that we shall turn now.

6 Where There's Muck There's Magic

HUMUS

The word humus is enough to bring tears of joy to the eyes of some gardeners. The dead and decaying plant material called humus has defied full analysis by soil scientists but it is known that when it is fully decayed it coats the soil particles.

One of the key things about humus is that it swells when wet and shrinks when dry which means that it is spongy and water-retaining. So when it rains the humus soaks up the water preventing the soil from becoming broken down and waterlogged.

In natural circumstances the plants and animals die, fall to the ground, decay and form humus. This cycle ensures that there is always enough of this material for life in the soil to continue. However, life in the garden is far from natural. Parts of plants, like leaves, flowers, fruits and seeds, are constantly being removed by gardeners. Whole plants are uprooted sometimes, especially in annual borders and in the vegetable plot. It is a truism to say, 'you can only get out what you put in' and this applies to soil too, the humus-making materials that are removed from the soil have to be compensated for in some way. The more the soil is cultivated the faster humus disappears because the bacteria that feed on the humus are stimulated by the tilling of the soil.

There are three main types of humus makers: raw humus, matured humus and fertilisers that add humus as an extra bonus.

FYM

Raw humus is not really humus at all because the material can still be recognised for what it is. It might include grass clippings, leaves, vegetable refuse from the garden and kitchen, seaweed, straw, dry bracken, pet litter, tea leaves, annual weeds (never perennial ones) and manure or, as they say in polite circles, FYM (Farm

Yard Manure). Whilst some of these could be used as they are to provide humus for soils it is not always advisable to do so because in this form they will stimulate bacterial action which will rob the soil of the plant food, nitrogen.

The value of manure to any gardener cannot be underestimated. It is a humus-provider *par excellence* and also a fertiliser, although the amounts contained are very small. FYM can be cow, horse or pig dung mixed with straw or other material that has been used under the animals to absorb the excreta. Of course the way the animal was fed, what litter material was used and how long the FYM was stored before use all play a part in deciding what value the manure has. For example, storage in an exposed place quickly reduces the plant food levels since rainwater leaches them out.

As a rule-of-thumb about 11 lb of FYM are needed per sq yd (5 kg per sq m) to bring about some beneficial effects to the soil. Usually horse dung is recognised as the richest FYM in terms of plant nutrition, pig dung contains less and cow dung the least.

Horse manure is the driest type and is very useful for improving clayey soils. It has also been used with great success for making mushroom beds and constructing hotbeds. A hotbed is a stack of manure on top of which soil or potting mixture is placed. It has been used for warming soils and producing out of season crops since Roman times. In eighteenth-century England, pineapples were cultured using hotbeds which maintained a soil temperature of up to 90°F (32°C) from March through to October. The reason for the phenomenal success of these hotbeds was the addition of 'tanbark', bark used in tanning. Unfortunately tanbark is no longer available.

Pig and cow manure have a closer texture more suited to improving light sandy soils. Some gardeners use cow manure in potting mixtures but first it is air-dried. Poultry manure is sometimes available and this is far richer in plant foods especially if dried. Believe it or not pigeon manure is utilised by some and this is even more fertile. Naturally such caustic materials should not be used fresh, they should either be stored or well mixed with soil or potting mixture first.

COMPOSING A COMPOST

Humus-providing materials are of most use when broken down and mature. The secret here is to compost the materials and composing a compost heap is as much an art as composing a symphony. Just as an orchestra consists of many instruments, all of which play their own tune and need to be drawn together by a conductor, so a compost heap is made of many ingredients and the gardener needs to organise them to get the best results.

No horticulturalist will ever be as exalted as Beethoven or Mozart!, but there are many local folk tales within every town, of the gardeners who could make a really good compost which is light, open, spongy and humus-rich.

Good, usable compost should be so decayed that – like all humus – it is no longer recognisable for what it originally was. It should be dark brown, moist, crumbly, very uniform in texture and have no offensive smell.

The bacteria that are responsible for breaking down the material can work in two ways, either they can use oxygen to live – aerobic respiration – or do without it – anaerobic respiration. Those who want compost quickly, aerobic composters, are prepared to be more vigilant, anaerobic composters are prepared to wait in return for not bothering with the heap while composing occurs.

Composting using the aerobic method produces a better end product. Additionally it will destroy all harmful forms of life, micro-organisms as well as weed seeds and plants, not smell unpleasant or be the object of attention for rats, mice and flies.

AEROBIC COMPOSTING

The minimum size of composting bin for a garden is about 1 cu yd (1 cu m). Any 'bin' smaller than this will not generate enough heat to kill pests, diseases and weed seeds. Wood, bricks or breeze blocks, or any material which provides good heat insulation, can be used to construct the bin.

Some gardeners use straw bales to make the linings for their compost bins as these are full of air and provide the best insulation. About once a year the bales need to be replaced as they get broken down along with the rest of the material. It is best if at least two bins are available so that one can be filled during the season whereas the other can be left undisturbed until it is fully composted and ready to use.

For the best aerobic compost the bacteria naturally present in the materials used must be stimulated by giving them air, moisture, a source of nitrogen and chalk.

Air can be incorporated into the compost by either providing a brick base with plenty of holes covered by

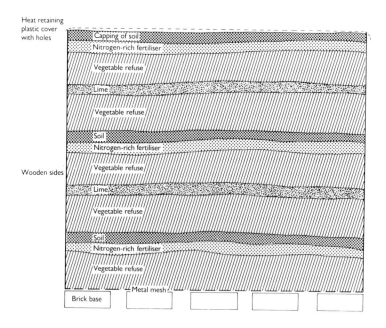

Figure 6.1 An Aerobic Compost Heap

metal mesh or by making the bottom layer of compost
consist of about 6 in (15 cm) of twigs and brushwood
(Figure 6.1).

Then the vegetable material can be added. Only
woody material, which will not decompose quickly
enough, and diseased plant stuff should not be used.
Cabbage stalks should be well chopped up or shredded if
they are to be used successfully. As a general rule
perennial weeds should not be used, unless they are
completely dead they will regenerate when put back on
to the garden.

Dry materials like bracken and straw can be composted
if they are well wetted first. Newspaper, pet litter and
other animal excreta all make useful additions to the
compost heap if not added in excess. Leaves can be
composted too but if large amounts are involved they are
best treated separately. Oak and beach leaves compost
better than, say, the thicker leaves of sycamore, and
plane, which resist decay for years.

Pine needles are also difficult to break down because
they are resin-filled and have a thick waxy cuticle around
them. Also they will produce a very acidic leaf mould
only suitable for calcifuges like *Rhododendron*.

Lawn clippings can be treated like leaves, either used in small amounts or composted separately. If the latter occurs the grass will turn into a foul-smelling, soggy mess unless kept to 6 in (15 cm) layers which are separated by 1 in (2.5 cm) layers of soil. These days proprietary 'recyclers' can be used to speed up the process; such chemicals supply the bacteria with nitrogen food. If plastic sheeting is put over the clippings the heat will be kept in and the air out; the outcome will be faster composting.

Although the compost heap should not be allowed to dry out, it should not be allowed to become saturated either. The layers of the compost 'sandwich' should be built up gradually, first the mixed vegetable refuse – about 6 in (15 cm) of it – then a thin layer of a nitrogen-rich fertiliser such as sulphate of ammonia, dried blood, animal manure or proprietary 'activator' or 'accelerator', then a covering of soil, then another layer of vegetable matter, then a covering of lime or powdered chalk.

The bacteria and fungi which will do the 'aerobics' need nitrogen food so the fertiliser is essential for efficient composting – this is especially true in the autumn and winter – and is covered with a layer of soil which will provide the bacteria and fungi needed. Limey materials are added to prevent an accumulation of acidic compounds which would slow down the rotting process. The fertiliser and lime should never be put into direct contact because they will react with one another and not do the jobs they were intended to do, so they are used in alternate layers (see Figure 6.1).

When the heap is complete the surface should be flattened off and capped with a layer of soil. On top of all this a heat-retaining layer, like straw or bracken or plastic with small holes in it, should be placed.

Usually the heap has to be 'turned', that is the outer layers are put into the centre, every couple of weeks if the gardener is energetic enough. At least one turning is essential unless straw bales have been used to line the bin because ony then will all the material be broken down. If the heap does become dry it is best to drive holes into it and pour in water. After as little as one month in summer and four months in winter the compost should be ready for use.

ANAEROBIC COMPOSTING

If all this sounds like too much trouble then anaerobic composting may be for you. As you might imagine from the name this method excludes air, and more particularly oxygen, from the material to be decomposed. It is very simple as well since all the material to be used is heaped together, 'the more the merrier', but it will look tidier placed in a bin constructed of wire netting, wood or both.

The anaerobic compost heap is not to be turned, which saves backache, and although nitrogen fertilisers – like ammonium sulphate – and lime can be added in alternate layers there really is no need for them. Within this heap there is little oxygen so the bacteria and fungi switch to breaking down their food without it. Unfortunately, there is not much energy to be gained from this so the rotting process is slow.

Composting this way can take up to one year but the products are just as good; uniform, dark, crumbly humus just ready to use in the garden. If compost is made with either the aerobic or anaerobic method it needs to be stored properly. If it is allowed to be exposed to the elements the plant foods will be washed out or leached. Either the material should be kept under a waterproof cover or in the shed or other building.

MULCHES

Once manures and composted material have been obtained the next step is to use them properly. Composts can be applied around the roots of plants when they are planted, a so-called 'base dressing'. Manures should not touch the roots or green parts of plants as they will be so toxic to the cells as to scorch the specimens. The answer is to use raw as well as mature, composted materials as mulches.

Traditionally, mulches are thick layers of organic materials laid on the surface of the soil. Any manure or compost can be used along with peat, pulverised (shredded) bark, spent hops, straw, mushroom compost and grass cuttings.

Mulches serve many functions. They conserve moisture within the soil allowing the plant roots to benefit from the moisture rather than allowing evaporation to carry water away into the air. If the mulch has any plant foods, as the manures do, then these will be leached down to the plant roots and generally help in plant growth.

Mulches exclude light from the soil and so prevent weed seeds germinating and thriving. Because of their dark colour they absorb all the available heat, this means that they keep the soil warmer in winter allowing good root protection. Also the soil surface beneath the mulch will be cooler in the summer, protected from the sun, which will encourage soil bacteria and discourage soil pests.

Unfortunately, however, not everything is marvellous about mulches. They absorb rainfall so plants are best watered well before the mulch is applied and after that watering needs to be well done or not done at all. Also the winter temperatures above the mulch material will be lower than those above bare soil if no mulch is applied. So, to take an example, the straw usually put around strawberry plants before they fruit means that although the fruits are unsoiled the flowers that precede them are more liable to frost damage so they have to be covered on cold nights.

In these modern times inorganic materials like black polythene and aluminium foil have been used as mulches. Although they do not have any plant foods to offer and can be unsightly, they offer every advantage of normal mulches. Additionally artificial mulches absorb the sun's heat, if they are dark, or reflect it, if they are light; either way they make the plants warm up and grow faster.

If slits are cut in the mulch, vegetables can be planted in these. In this way weed growth is made practically impossible because of the lack of light. A warning, though, the ground needs to be watered thoroughly before an artificial mulch is laid otherwise the plants will suffer a severe drought and may die as a result.

PEAT

Substances like peat contain little if any plant foods. The two types of peat commonly available are *Sphagnum* moss and sedge peat. All peats are made from partially decayed plant matter; because of the acidic, wet places where they are found full decay never takes place.

Sedge peat is the remains of marsh plants like reeds, sedges, heathers, mosses and even tree roots. On the other hand *Sphagnum* moss is made entirely from this peat bog moss. So, although peat may just be described as 'peat moss' there are two very different types with different properties.

The pH of sedge peat can be anything between 3.5 and 7.0 (very acidic through to neutral) and it can hold up to eight times its own weight of water. *Sphagnum* peat is always acidic, between pH 3.5 to 4.0, and is a 'living sponge' able to hold up to fifteen times its own weight of water.

Peats make excellent soil conditioners but since sedge peat contains more nitrogen, which is a source of food for bacteria, it is more easily broken down. So although both types are good for improving soils, *Sphagnum* peat is often used in planting holes to help establish roots and also dug into clay soils. The water within the moss expands when frozen and helps to break up the clay clods of earth. Sedge peat makes a useful mulch as it is dark and absorbs the sun's heat.

As peats are generally acidic they also make ideal materials for use in beds where calcifuges like heathers (*Calluna*) are to make their home. Otherwise if less extreme soil conditions are required an application of lime will neutralise the acidity. A simple pH test will confirm whether enough lime has been added.

Tremendous amounts of peat have to be used in order to bring about changes in the condition of a soil. At least $4\frac{1}{2}$ lb per sq yd (2 kg per sq m) are needed in average soils to keep them 'in trim', but if the soil is particularly sandy or otherwise lacks organic matter then about 11 lb (5 kg) should be used in the same area and lightly worked into the surface. The finer the peat particles the better it is at keeping moisture in when used as a mulch and here about 10 lb (4.5 kg) is about right per sq yd (sq m).

Peat is an invaluable material to the modern horticulturalist. It can be used to improve the texture of soil, as a mulch, in planting holes for trees and shrubs, as a compost of seed and potting mixtures, to provide the acidic conditions needed by calcifuges and even become a major part of bulb fibre so that daffodils, tulips and crocuses can be brought indoors to flower.

Before any peat is used it must be thoroughly wetted and if it is a part of seed and potting mixtures it is best not to let it dry out. A dried peat mix can be very difficult to rewet and, as anyone who has experienced this will confirm, when peat dries it shrinks away from the sides of the container so that when water is applied it tends to flow down the side cracks rather than pass through the peat mix.

Apart from raw humus, like grass clippings, and mature humus, which has been composted, the organic part of the soil can be augmented by green manure and organic fertilisers. Green manure is a crop grown purely for digging into the soil to improve the humus content.

The cheap and easily grown mustard (*Sinapis alba*) is commonly used. Seeds sown in August are allowed to grow and dug into the soil during the autumn. In chalky and sandy soils it is a useful green manure but to prevent a shortage of nitrogen for plants which follow, because bacteria will use this food to help break down the manure, it is necessary to apply a nitrogen fertiliser before sowing the mustard.

Only fertilisers like 'hoof and horn', 'fish meal', dried blood, seaweed, bone meal and animal manure all provide humus as well as plant foods. It is to these plant foods that we are to turn now.

7 Food, Glorious Food

A HEALTHY DIET

Just as people need a balanced diet to keep them healthy and fit so do plants. However, there is one important difference, whereas people rely on a complex mixture of proteins, fats, sugars, minerals, vitamins and water, plants have much simpler needs. Green plants have the unique and wonderful ability to capture sunlight and, with the aid of carbon dioxide gas from the air and water and minerals from the soil, manufacture sugars.

Photosynthesis is the process that welds these materials together to make sugars and in turn these can be used to make all the materials that plants need to make new leaves, stems and roots. But, just as people grow and thrive when fed on a diet containing all the essential ingredients, so do plants – and fertilisers aim to provide extra minerals.

In a natural situation the minerals found in the soil provide all the plant's needs and as the plant roots remove them they are replaced by the decaying plants and animals that become incorporated into the soil. But in the very unnatural garden situation the reserves of minerals run out quickly unless replaced by the use of fertilisers.

The fertiliser advertisements are full of jargon like 'NPK', 'compound', 'straight', 'organic', 'inorganic' and 'liquid' fertilisers. What do they all mean and what do they contain?

Perhaps the best way to answer this is to talk about their content first. All fertiliser bags, packets and containers have the same three letters inscribed on them, NPK.

'THE BIG THREE' – NITROGEN, PHOSPHATES AND POTASH

N stands for nitrogen. Some gardeners call it 'the leaf maker' because of its ability to promote leaf growth

(Table 7.1). It is especially good for any crop grown for its leaves, such as cabbage and lettuce. Grasses benefit too, so lawns look much better a few days after an appliation of nitrogen.

Plants suffering from lack of nitrogen have small, pale stunted green leaves and stems. On the other hand too much causes soft, sappy growth which easily collapses.

Although the air is about 80 per cent nitrogen this is of no direct use to plants, they rely on the nitrate compounds in the soil. Sandy soils are so well drained that most plant foods, including the nitrates, are leached out.

A few lucky plants have other plants living within them that can capture nitrogen from the air, fix it in chemical form and then pass it on to the plant. A few bacteria, blue-green algae and fungi can 'fix' atmospheric nitrogen as they live in the soil. Most important they can invade larger plants in order to obtain protection and a supply of foods for themselves and as they do so the host plant obtains a free source of nitrates.

Some mosses, ferns, duckweeds and even the giant 'prickly rhubarb' (*Gunnera manicata*) have blue-green algae in their roots. Alder (*Alnus* species) and other woody plants have nitrogen-fixing bacteria to help them.

Once again it is the flowering plants that seem to have the most efficient association. Most use a bacterium called *Rhizobium*. As it enters the roots in large numbers it irritates the host plant so much that swellings, or nodules, form. The bacteria live within nodules and provide a free supply of nitrate foods for the plant. One flowering plant family which has benefited more than any other from this companionship is the pea and bean family (the *Papilionaceae*).

The great thing about nitrogen-fixation by plants living together in this way is that they do not need nitrogen fertilisers during their lifetime. Also, an added bonus, the crops that follow them need less nitrogen too. The algae, bacteria and fungi are no sluggards – between them they can fix over 100 lb of nitrogen per acre (110 kg per ha). This is the rough equivalent of applying over 1 ton per acre (2.5 tonnes per ha) of nitrogen fertiliser. If it were possible to gather together all of the nitrogen fixed by bacteria in the world's plants every year it would weigh about 100 million tons (tonnes).

All soils contain bacteria which exist by breaking down organic matter. Through a chain of chemical reactions brought about by a series of different bacteria nitrates are made. Although unseen, bacteria are as vital to the fertility of the soil as sand and clay.

Table 7.1 Fertiliser Ingredients and Their Uses

	Nutrients	Main Users	Symptoms of Deficiency
The Big Three	N – Nitrogen	Leafy crops. Grasses.	Small, stunted, pale leaves.
	P_2O_5 – Phosphates	Root vegetables.	Small, stunted plants with poorly developed roots.
	K_2O – Potash	Any flowers and fruits.	Leaves scorched at edges. Poor flowering and fruiting.
Two Important Allies	Ca – Calcium	All plants.	Small stunted plants with yellow leaves and short roots.
	Mg – Magnesium	All plants, especially rose flowers and tomatoes.	Pale or yellowed areas between leaf veins.
The Trace Elements	Fe – Iron Mn–Manganese S – Sulphur B – Boron Cu – Copper Mo – Molybdenum Zn – Zinc Co – Cobalt	All plants.	Rare to see this deficiency. Yellowing between leaf veins. Stunted growth.

The next major plant food are the phosphates (Table 7.1). These are usually represented as P or P_2O_5. Many gardeners call phosphate the 'root maker' and it certainly does stimulate the growth and development of root systems. Too little phosphate and the plant roots are few and stunted. The crops that need high levels of phosphates are ones that have large roots like parsnips and carrots.

The third member of the 'big three' plant foods is potash (Table 7.1). This is variously represented as K or K_2O and often described as the 'flower and fruit maker'. If there is insufficient potash plants do not grow properly, they are soft and weak and unable to form flowers and fruit. Plants suffering from a lack of potash show 'scorching' around the edge of their leaves.

Flowers like *Hippeastrum* do much better if given extra potash and other plants that store food in stems, like potatoes, or fruits, like tomatoes, all benefit from potash fertilisers. It appears that potash stimulates the sexual growth of plants, that is the production of flower buds, rather than the vegetative growth of leaves and shoots. Interestingly, potash is also known to give fruit a better flavour, so add potash for juicy fruit.

Phosphates and potash are just like nitrates in that they can be easily leached out of the soil by rainfall especially in stony, sandy and chalky areas.

Fertiliser containers always show how much NP and K they contain by a code written on the packaging. For example, National Growmore Fertiliser has the code 7:7:7 that is, 7 per cent Nitrogen; 7 per cent Phosphate; 7 per cent Potash by weight. The bigger the percentage figures the more food there is per unit weight and consequently less needs to be applied. Although it is a great temptation to overdose with cheap fertilisers, the recommended rate should never be exceeded because at best such action will scorch the foliage and at worst it might kill your plants.

TWO IMPORTANT ALLIES – CALCIUM AND MAGNESIUM

Two plant foods are needed in moderate amounts in order that garden plants can grow well; calcium (Ca) and magnesium (Mg). That very useful substance called lime is a source of calcium (Table 7.1).

Strictly speaking, lime is calcium oxide which is such a caustic material that it is rarely used in the garden. Though it is slower acting, hydrated or slaked lime, i.e. calcium oxide that has had water added to it, is often used in horticulture. Slowest acting of all, but in no immediate danger of scorching foliage, is ground chalk or limestone. Magnesian limestone not only provides calcium but magnesium too.

Beware of applying lime just because the plants need calcium, after all there are many choice plants like *Rhododendron* and *Camellia* that do their level best to avoid lime. In fact, the lime-haters, calcifuges, seem to be quite happy growing where there is no calcium available to them.

If soil acidity is not desired then lime is very useful for bringing about its reduction. After a pH test has been done to determine the acidity of the soil, the amount of lime required, if any, can be calculated (Table 7.2).

Table 7.2 Amounts of Hydrated Lime Needed to Raise the pH Level to 6.5. lb per sq yd (kg per sq m)

Original pH	Clay or Peat lb	(kg)	Medium Loam lb	(kg)	Gravelly or Sandy Soils lb	(kg)
4.0	5	(2.3)	4½	(2.0)	3½	(1.6)
4.5	4	(1.8)	3½	(1.6)	3	(1.4)
5.0	3¼	(1.5)	2¾	(1.2)	2¼	(1.0)
5.5	2¼	(1.0)	2	(0.9)	1¼	(0.7)
6.0	1½	(0.7)	1	(0.5)	½	(0.3)

Apart from reducing acidity in soil lime also acts to encourage the bacteria that convert nitrogen to nitrates, the plant foods of so much importance. Earthworms also multiply best in limed soil and the clay particles are flocculated by the action of lime. Both these processes help to keep the soil well aerated and drained.

Lime can be applied to vacant ground at any time of the year but autumn is the usual time for clay soils and spring for sandy soils. It can be scattered over the surface or lightly worked into the surface with a hoe or rake.

Potting mixtures generally have lime in them, even peat-based ones, so if calcifuges are to be grown a special lime-free mix must be used. Also beware of some fertilisers that contain calcium which can make the soil conditions alkaline.

Magnesium is the second food needed in moderate amounts by most plants and in large quantities by some like tomatoes and roses. A lack of magnesium leads to leaves which have yellow areas between the veins because this element is needed to make the green pigment chlorophyll. Well-drained soils often have plants suffering from this disease, known as chlorosis. Interestingly, if too much potash is given to crops they often exhibit chlorosis and the cure is to apply a solution of Epsom Salt (magnesium sulphate) which contains 10 per cent magnesium.

THE TRACE ELEMENTS

Only minute amounts of other elements are needed by healthy plants. These include iron (Fe), manganese (Mn), sulphur (S), boron (B), copper (Cu), molybdenum (Mo), zinc (Zn) and cobalt (Co). Although only a few parts per million are required, a deficiency or over-abundance of these materials can devastate a crop. Fortunately soils usually have sufficient of these trace elements to cope with most situations and fertilisers used for specialised crops usually also provide the necessary trace elements.

ORGANIC VERSUS INORGANIC FERTILISERS

There is a long-standing debate between some gardeners who believe that organic fertilisers, those of animal and plant origins, are preferable to inorganic ones, those manufactured. Indeed, the air turns as blue as a *Meconopsis grandis* (Blue Poppy) when these two parties get together.

As might be expected there is a part to be played by both natural and artificial fertilisers and since their jobs are somewhat different they can be complementary and not alternatives.

Organic fertilisers are slow-acting and best added to the soil just before planting. Their big advantage is that they release plant foods over a long period of time. Since only small amounts of organic fertilisers are applied at any one time they provide very small quantities of humus. This means that they are good for providing plant foods but are poor soil conditioners.

Inorganic fertilisers are quick-release products designed to give plants an immediate source of nutrients. They are of most use when worked into the surface of the soil – a top dressing – or sprayed directly on to the leaves as a foliar feed.

Just to show you how futile the organic versus inorganic battle is, consider what it is that plant roots absorb. It is the very fine root hairs that extend from the main root that take in the vast majority of foods. They do so using three processes; diffusion, cation exchange and active transport.

Diffusion is a simple but effective process. Because there are usually many more nutrients outside the root than inside it, there is a tendency for them to drift into it.

Many believe that plant roots exchange hydrogen ions (charged hydrogen particles) for plant foods and this is called cation exchange. This has drastic long-term consequences because although the plants obtain badly needed foods the soil obtains a high concentration of hydrogen ions. In other words the pH decreases, the soil becomes more acidic and sour.

Plants need foods from the soil so much that they will use energy to get them. Dragging in foods means that they become much more concentrated inside the plant and the natural tendency is for them to drift out again, by diffusion. Plants need to do two things, move some into the transport tissues to get it out of the root, and also use energy to keep it in the root and stop it flowing back out to the soil again. The latter process is called active transport.

Plant foods can only get into the plant if they are in mineral or inorganic form. No matter what kind of fertiliser is used it really makes no difference to the plant – if it is to take up the food it must be in inorganic form. So you see even if organic fertilisers are used, when they break down it is the inorganic part that the roots absorb. What is more, the so-called inorganic fertiliser ammonium sulphate is usually ultimately made from wood.

TYPES OF FERTILISERS

By now we know the diet that plants need but how should the food be given? Apart from a bewildering choice or inorganic and organic compounds there are also straight, compound, liquid and solid fertilisers.

Straight fertilisers contain, mainly, one of the three major plant foods. There are organic fertilisers like dried blood, bone meal, fish meal, wood ashes, hoof and horn and guano (Table 7.3). Inorganic fertilisers include ammonium sulphate, superphosphate, potassium sulphate (sulphate of potash), calcium cyanamide, iron sulphate, potassium nitrate, magnesium sulphate, nitrate of soda, nitro-chalk, potassium phosphate (phosphate of potash) and so on (Table 7.4).

Compound fertilisers contain all three major plant foods so this is a much more convenient way of giving a general feed to all plants. So-called 'general' compound fertilisers contain roughly the same amounts of N, P and K, whereas 'specific' compound fertilisers are made to suit one plant or group of plants. For example, rose and tomato fertilisers are high in potash but lawn compounds have plenty of nitrogen; the former encourages flowers and fruit whereas the latter helps production of leaves.

Table 7.3 Understanding the Organics

Fertiliser	Content	Uses
Dried blood	10-13% N	Any leafy vegetable, e.g. cabbages.
Bone meal	20-30% P_2O_5 1-5% N + calcium	Trees, shrubs, vines. **NB** Make sure it is sterilised.
Fish meal	7-10% N 5-15% P_2O_5 2-3% K_2O	Buried one spit deep long before sowing or planting.
Hoof and horn	7-15% N 1-10% P_2O_5 + calcium	A pre-planting ferti- liser for all crops and in planting mixtures.
Guano	10-14% N 9-11% P_2O_5 2-4% K_2O	A useful top-dressing and constituent of planting mixes.
Wood ashes	1-7% K_2O	For any flowers or fruit

Many gardeners prefer liquid rather than solid fertilisers. Because they are dissolved in water liquid feeds
can be watered on to the soil immediately above the roots
or sprayed on to the leaves, or both.

Many liquid fertilisers on offer today are called foliar
feeds because they are designed specifically for spraying
on leaves and shoots. The most effective way of applying
these is on the underside of the leaves since this is where
most of the stomata (holes) are to be found and also
usually where the cuticle, or waxy coat, is thinner and
allows the feed to enter. In this way the feed reaches the
plant cells much quicker than by using other means and
so the plant responds within a few hours.

Just as the soil around plants needs to be watered
before applying liquid fertilisers the same is true when
using solid fertilisers. After all, the food needs to be
taken to the roots and the only way of doing this is to
make sure there is plenty of water to carry it there. Both
liquid and solid fertilisers are available as straight, single
crop use, or compound, general use, formulations.

Table 7.4 Understanding the Inorganics

Fertiliser	Content	Uses
Ammonium sulphate	20.6% N + sulphur	Brassicas and potatoes. Acidifies soils.
Superphosphate	13-18% P_2O_5	Before sowing or planting. Triple super-phosphate has $2\frac{1}{2}$ times as much P_2O_5.
Potassium sulphate	48% K_2O	For flowers and fruit. Acidifies soils.
Potassium phosphate	51% P_2O_5 36% K_2O	Expensive but very useful as a liquid feed for all flowers.
Magnesium sulphate	10% Mg + sulphur	To avoid or cure chlorosis.
Sodium nitrate	16% N + trace elements	Leaves and stems of any plants.
Nitro-chalk	15.5% N + calcium	Long-lasting and very useful on acid soils before sowing, planting or during growth.
Iron sulphate	Fe + S	Cures iron-induced chlorosis. Acidifies soils. Kills fungi and mosses (ingredient of lawn sand).
Potassium nitrate	12-14% N 44-46% K_2O	A good general fertiliser. Chilean potassium nitrate is only 10% K_2O.

TOO MUCH OR TOO LITTLE FOOD

Although plants have a demand for all major and minor plant foods that does not, of course, mean that they will get them. In acidic conditions (any pH less than 7) nitrogen, phosphates, potash and many other foods are less available to plants (Figure 7.1). Bacteria and earthworms are also in smaller numbers and in extremely acidic conditions, they may disappear completely. Equally, in alkaline conditions phosphates, calcium, magnesium and many minor foods are more difficult to find as far as plant roots are concerned.

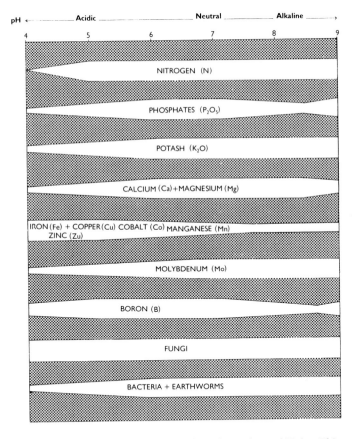

Figure 7.1 The Availability of Plant Foods and Numbers of Living Things in Soils of Different pHs. The broader the band the more there is

Assuming the pH of your soil is not too acidic or alkaline then normally no plant foods should be unavailable and the occasional reinforcement of major and minor foods will be beneficial. However, too much can be a bad thing. If too much lime is applied iron and magnesium will become 'locked up', the plant will be unable to make enough chlorophyll and the leaves will become yellow. Application of sequestered or chelated compounds called sequestrols will remedy this lime-induced chlorosis.

CARNIVOROUS PLANTS

Whatever foods are absorbed they all go to fire the chemical reactions that lead to growth and development of the plant. Some very specialised flowering plants live in soils which are so deficient in nutrients, and especially nitrates, that they have to look elsewhere for food. They have become flesh-eaters.

There are over 400 species of carnivorous plants in the world but probably the most widely known is the Venus Fly Trap (*Dionaea muscipula*). The modified leaf of this plant is flattened into a two-lobed blade, the two halves of which form a right angle with the midrib at the centre. Each leaf lobe bears stiff spines across its margin and on its upper surface three sensitive trigger-hairs stand erect. The upper surface also bears red glandular hairs which increase in number as the leaf matures, hence a deeper red appears.

Insects, flies and beetles mostly, are attracted to the sweet-tasting nectar at the base of the spines and the trap is sprung by the scavenging insect when one or more of the trigger-hairs are touched. In less than a quarter of a second the two leaf lobes close to meet each other, their spines interlock to prevent the prey's escape and then – here the squeamish can skip the rest of the paragraph – the lobes squeeze together slowly. Now the glandular hairs discharge a fluid which digests the greater part of the animal leaving only the indigestible husk behind. All this takes about three days and the leaf re-opens and awaits the arrival of the next victim.

For the impatient these traps can be sprung with a matchstick or even with a hair but too many false alarms will weaken the plant. The traps eventually die but will be replaced throughout the summer and if placed in a sunny position clusters of white flowers will be produced which contrast well with the red leaves. Normally the fading flowers should be removed so that seed production does not sap the plant's energy.

Sundews are plants which belong to the same plant family as the Venus Fly Trap, the *Droseraceae*, but their foliage is quite different. The leaves are covered by glandular tentacles which are longer on the leaf margins and shorter in the centre. These tentacles each carry a drop of fluid which sparkles in the sunlight, hence the name of 'sundew'.

The whole leaf surface is as sticky as flypaper because of the fluid produced by small glands on the leaf. An insect attracted to the leaves by their appearance soon becomes enmeshed in the fluids. The more the animal struggles the more entangled it becomes.

Now the horror story really begins as the tentacles curve inward and deliver their digestive juices. Slowly the insect becomes suffocated by the fluids and the digestive processes dissolve all but the husk of the prey which remains as a deadly advertisement to others that it is 'safe' to alight on this plant.

Sundews vary tremendously in size. Pygmy sundews are only $\frac{3}{4}$ inch (2 cm) across whereas the tuberous sundews of western Australia are the nearest thing to the mythical animated plants called Triffids that you are likely to encounter as they are climbers, anything up to 3 ft (1 m) high.

Some gardeners believe that there is nothing as pretty as a pitcher. The pitchers referred to are modified leaves which in the tropical *Nepenthes* species consist of a midrib which is extended as a tendril which expands at the end into a hollow vessel. In the more familiar North American *Sarracenia* species the whole of the leaf is modified into a long conical container which is closed by a lid when young. Such pitchers vary in height from 6 to 36 in (15 to 100 cm) depending on the species.

Flies and other insects are attracted to the plants by sweet nectar produced on the lid, lip and throat of the pitchers. Once attracted over the run these animals lose their foothold on the very smooth wall of the throat which is made up of minute waxy scales which slide freely over one another. The prey plunges into a deadly soup at the bottom of the well. *Sarracenia* plants make retreat even more unlikely by growing downward-pointing hairs inside the pitcher.

The juices of the cauldron immobilise the insects and then digest the soft parts of the body leaving only the husks as a reminder of their former fatal mistake and grim ending. With such an efficient weapon it is not surprising that each pitcher can deal with up to 10,000 victims each year.

Butterworts, the *Pinguiculas*, have broad yellow, green, oval-shaped leaves which are oily to the touch. This is due to glands on the upper leaf surfaces which release a glue capable of apprehending even the most fleet-footed insect. Worse news awaits the captured animals for between these structures are different glands which make lethal digestive fluids. Once trapped the insects are slowly digested and, like sundews, the husks remain to invite others to land and meet the same sticky end on this 'floral flypaper'.

These and other carnivorous plants can become a passion for some gardeners. Since they are accustomed to nitrogen-deficient locations, when cultivated in the home the same conditions must be provided. They need a potting mixture of *Sphagnum* peat and when watering always use rainwater or distilled water (cooled water from the kettle or melted ice from the ice box will do) and never, NEVER, give them fertilisers of any sort.

Whatever method is used to obtain foods, using roots or carnivorous leaves, if the right amounts are absorbed the results are the same, actively growing plants. In order to provide extra protection many gardeners have resorted to using greenhouses. It is this aspect that we shall consider next.

8 Protect and Survive

GROWING UNDER GLASS

Glasshouses, low plastic tunnels, walk-in tunnels, cloches and frames are all methods of protecting plants from cold temperatures. They enable a far greater range of plants to be grown and much more besides.

Protective structures can be utilised for seven main roles. First, many plants, including vegetables like cabbages and cauliflowers as well as flowers, including the half-hardy annuals and perennials, can be raised from seed and grown on until they are a suitable size for bedding outside.

Secondly, plants can be multiplied, or propagated, easily using glasshouses and related structures. This leads on to the third role, that of displaying flowering and foliage pot plants. Many gardeners prefer to display their prize flowers inside the home so greenhouses can be used for cut flower production too. Many tender plants, those that frost will kill, can be grown out-of-season. Often gardeners will crop lettuce during the winter months by using a glasshouse. Lastly, the seventh role, tender food crops like tomatoes, melons and cucumbers can be successfully cultivated inside a protective structure.

What is it that makes greenhouses so good for all these jobs? The answer is that within the structure a special environment or micro-climate is created which is generally beneficial to plant growth.

Surprisingly the light intensity, the strength of light, is lower inside a greenhouse than outside it. As sunlight passes through glass not all of it makes the journey into the 'house'. Some of it is absorbed by the material. In order that the maximum amount of light energy does pass through it is vital that the glass is kept clean, especially during the winter months. On the other hand, the summer sunrays can be a positive embarrassment to the aspiring gardener and so shading may become necessary.

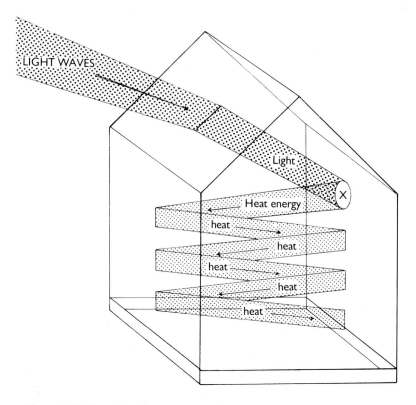

Figure 8.1 Why a Greenhouse Heats Up. Light waves pass through the glass and strike objects within the structure (X). These objects give off heat energy which cannot pass back through the glass and so there is a build-up of heat energy and the temperature rises

The temperatures experienced inside protective structures are usually higher than those outside. This is again due to sunlight (Figure 8.1). The light passes through the glass and strikes objects inside the glasshouse. These objects radiate heat energy which warms the air and other things within the structure. The big difference is that heat cannot penetrate the glass or other material and so the greenhouse warms up.

Air turbulence is lessened inside protective structures. Only when the ventilators and doors are open, can air move reasonably well. In more normal circumstances the air inside greenhouses moves very little and this can prove disastrous because increased temperatures and humidity are two potential plant killers.

The higher temperatures encourage greater transpiration (water loss) from the plants. Even though well-watered plants will try to replace transpired water they may not be able to do it quickly enough. Not surprisingly leaves and shoots start to wilt. Since the tips of the stems receive water preferentially then it is the lower leaves that suffer, they dry up and fall. As the condition spreads other leaves display brown spots or tips or edges. Flowers also drop when water is short.

It does not rain inside greenhouses. This may seem obvious but it does mean that water within the structure comes from two main sources. First, there is the transpired water from plant shoots and secondly, there is water introduced by people, mains water of one sort or another.

Increased humidity can lead to an increase in fungal infections and pest outbreaks too. Warm air can hold much more water than colder air. This is because the air molecules move around more when heat is applied and as they get further apart there is space for water molecules. As heat is withdrawn, the air cools, and the air 'jiggles about' less leaving less space for water.

In the hot house there is plenty of room for water, whereas outside it there could be cooler, drier air – so what happens when the two air masses meet? It is the glass, or plastic, that presents a barrier to both types of air and so it can be warmed on one side and cooled on the other.

Once warm air is cooled on the surface of the glazing material it loses its ability to carry water and so droplets form on the surface. As these droplets gather and coalesce small streams of condensation run down the glass. If these miniature rivers touch plants the outcome is a catastrophe, usually fungal infections followed by death.

High humidity is a blessing to some plants; ferns (like *Adiantum*), azaleas (*Rhododendron*) and umbrella plants (*Cyperus*) all prefer a wet tropical environment.

If the reverse is made possible, where ventilators are kept open whenever reasonable, then a different range of plants can be successfully cultivated. The spider plant (*Chlorophytum comosum variegatum*), cacti and succulents, ornamental figs (*Ficus*) and *Eucalyptus* would be more at home in dry air conditions.

Even if the gardener possesses no greenhouse it is as well to remember how conditions vary inside such structures because the same is true of other structures, whether it be the humble cloche or even in various rooms within the home.

Any sunny position, even a south-facing window sill, is suitable for a whole range of specimens including *Acacia, Bougainvillea, Celosia, Heliotropium, Jasminum, Nerine, Passiflora, Pelargonium, Rosa* and *Zebrina* (Table 8.1).

Table 8.1 Pick-a-position then Pick-a-plant

Position	Suitable Plants
Sunny (south facing)	*Acacia, Agapanthus, Bougainvillea, Celosia, Heliotropium, Jasminum, Nerine, Passiflora, Pelargonium, Rosa* and *Zebrina*
Partially sunny (east or west facing)	*Beloperone, Capsicum, Chlorophytum, Chrysanthemum, Ficus, Gynura, Impatiens, Poinsettia, Saintpaulia, Sansevieria* and *Tradescantia.*
Partially shaded (near north-facing window)	*Dracaena (fragrans* and *marginata)*, *Fatshedera, Fatsia, Ferns, Hedera, Howea, Maranta, Neanthe* and *Scindapsus.*
Shaded (away from any direct light source, e.g. window)	*Aglaonema, Aspidistra, Asplenium, Fittonia, Helxine, Philodendron, Pellionia* and *Tolmiea.* Only foliage – *never* flowering plants here.

Note: Remember that most plants that need partially sunny conditions will tolerate less light for a short period of time and vice versa.

If the greenhouse is shaded, or a room facing away from any direct sunlight is found, only plants able to cope with lower levels of light can be grown. These might include *Aspidistra Fittonia, Helxine* and *Philodendron*.

There are, of course, conditions which lie somewhere in between and the key thing is to make sure that the prevailing heat, humidity and light are matched to the plants to be cultivated.

Also there are many styles of greenhouse (Figure 8.2) which try to achieve the optimum conditions for growth. Only the gardener can decide how much space, headroom, heat and so on are needed and make a decision as to which is best. Whatever type is chosen the angle of the roof to the horizontal must be more than 20° or condensation drips will bring disaster to greenhouse plants.

Apart from light, warmth and humidity potential buyers should consider the stability, accessibility and maintenance problems too. No greenhouse is worth considering if it is likely to disappear into the next-door neighbour's garden during windy conditions. The door(s)

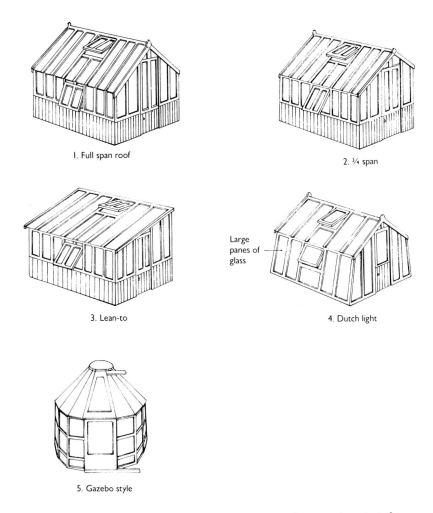

1. Full span roof

2. ¾ span

3. Lean-to

Large panes of glass

4. Dutch light

5. Gazebo style

Figure 8.2 Greenhouses. The glass may be down to the ground or start above the wood or brick level. In the former, there is more light and in the latter, there is more heat retained

need to be wide enough to allow a wheelbarrow and maybe an invalid chair into the greenhouse.

Lastly, modern materials have been used to reduce the maintenance required by gardeners. Mild steel is often used for hollow structural members which support the majority of the 'house' which is made of aluminium alloy. Whilst the steel needs protection from rust, and so is coated with zinc, the aluminium does not. If the two metals touch during damp conditions an electric current is generated, the zinc travels from the steel and is deposited on the aluminium. The steel then rusts and becomes another victim of electrolytic corrosion. So it is vital that the two are kept apart by oil or better still plastic.

Talking about plastic, glass has been made obsolete in many protective structures by a whole range of other materials. There is polythene (actually polythene chloride), PVC (polyvinylchloride) film, 'Melinex' polyester film and polypropylene rigid sheets.

It is important to remember that each of these materials will vary in terms of how they transmit light, allow it to pass through them, how they degrade with light and become opaque, how they transmit heat (the less the better) and how permeable they are to gases, if at all. Each crop has different requirements and will need different glazing materials.

HEATING YOUR GREENHOUSE

Heat travels in three main ways; convection, conduction and radiation. It does not matter if the heat is inside a house, greenhouse or in the garden the mechanisms are always the same.

Take convection, for example. If cream is poured into a hot cup of coffee the hot liquid rises and as it cools it sinks and is replaced by hotter coffee.

This movement occurs because extra heat moves the water and coffee molecules around faster and as they move they get further apart. Since the molecules are further apart the hot mixture becomes less dense and rises. As it does so the coffee loses heat energy, the molecules move apart less and become more dense and consequently it falls.

The coffee continues rising, cooling and sinking until it is all at a uniform cool temperature. By this time the cream is mixed in and the coffee changes from 'black' to 'white'.

Not only does this happen to liquids but convection currents are to be found in gases too. Air is a mixture of gases and hot air rises and cool air falls. Whatever form of heating is used in greenhouses the heat is carried through the air using convection currents.

Fumigation relies on convection too. Usually this process involves heating a solid or liquid compound which forms a vapour as it does so. Smoke cones and volatisers do this. The hot vapour moves through the air until it cools and becomes deposited on the plant foliage.

Conduction is the movement of heat energy from hotter to cooler objects. In the greenhouse this heat moves from the heater directly to the soil, staging, and so on or indirectly by passing into convection currents first and on to solid objects which are then heated. Heat is best retained in the greenhouse by using thermal screens or transparent plastic film linings which are bad conductors of heat.

This property of conduction is important for other processes inside the greenhouse. Automatic controllers fitted to individual ventilators are often filled with fluid which conducts the heat from the air well and expands rapidly as it does so to push a piston and open the vent.

Extractor fans often work by using bimetallic strips, two different metals which expand at different rates when they conduct the heat from the air. When they heat up they move apart, when they cool they touch, an electrical contact is made and the extractor fan switches on to remove the hot air. The maximum temperature which can be tolerated by most plants is 75°F (24°C).

Radiation involves the passage of heat through air just as the sun's heat falls on the earth. Surprisingly, air does not need to be present for radiation to occur. There is no air in outer space, but the sun's heat continues to fall.

If plants need to cool down transpiration comes to the rescue. By opening the stomata, the holes on the leaf surfaces, the extra water which evaporates takes heat energy with it. The leaf surface cools as a result. Sometimes in artificial environments Nature needs a helping hand. In greenhouses the surfaces of all the paving and staging can be 'damped down' or sprayed with water and the resulting evaporation takes heat from the 'house' and cools it as a result.

THE HISTORY OF GREENHOUSES

With thermostatic control and automatic ventilation, shading and watering, today's greenhouses are very different from those of the past. The first protective structures used were probably Roman buildings glazed with thin layers of mica. This is still a subject of debate but what is certain is that glass bell jars were used 400 years ago by French gardeners in order to protect their plants. In fact today we use the French word for bell, 'cloche'.

Unfortunately, the only way of providing ventilation to a glass cloche was to tilt them up on one side. This led to many crashes of glass and much hard work. Crashes occurred when the cloches shattered and hard work was made for some because as the wind changed direction someone had to turn the bell jars around.

By 1629 the use of cloches had spread to Britain and they were used for protecting melons. But, such an effective but inefficient method of protecting plants had to be improved on – and indeed it was. Its successor was the greenhouse, literally meaning a house to protect the 'greens'.

In the seventeenth century this meant that the tender shrubs and trees could be protected during the winter and brought out during the summer to enhance the garden. Many 'greenhouses' of this time were no more than south-facing wall gardens – already a well-known protective structure – which were roofed and glazed only on their south side.

Later, stoves were added in order to provide winter heat or topping-up warmth in the spring and autumn. Also, by the end of the seventeenth century, cold frames and conservatories were becoming commonplace.

The eighteenth and nineteenth centuries saw to it that the inside of greenhouses became lighter, with larger panes and smaller, stronger supports. The size of structure grew too. The most celebrated greenhouse was that built by Joseph Paxton at Chatsworth House in Derbyshire.

The doors allowed a carriage and four horses to be driven through with ease. Certainly Queen Victoria was impressed by what she saw, for here the banana and the giant water lily (*Victoria amazonica*) flowered for the first time in Britain. Unfortunately this massive monument to scientific gardening was to burn down. Paxton was to impress his rivals by designing Crystal Palace, but even this was to age and decay.

Today the Palm House at the Royal Botanic Gardens at Kew is the best large nineteenth-century glasshouse to be found in Britain. It was designed by Decimus Burton and completed in the late 1840s. Not only did the British have the splendid Palm House but they also developed the 6 × 4 ft (2 × 1.3 m) garden frame or 'light'. Only recently have glass and then plastic Dutch lights superseded the unwieldly frames.

The computer-controlled 'micro-chip' commercial greenhouses of today owe everything to their predecessors. Sensors constantly monitor the weather, including wind direction and humidity, and move ventilators and shading accordingly. Often no potting mixture is to be found in these structures. Tomatoes, for example, are commonly grown in gently sloping hydroponic troughs filled with water and plant foods, the levels of which are once again regulated by computers, and if the weather becomes dull supplementary lighting is automatically brought in to provide enough light to keep the plants growing at top speed. There is no guess work with this gardening.

The twentieth century has so far seen incredible developments in technology. By 1912 a continuous cloche was designed and within the last ten years the expanding cloche has come to light (forgive the irresistible pun). The latter cloche is a length of transparent plastic sheeting perforated with tiny slits. When first laid on the ground the slits are closed keeping moisture and heat in the soil. As the seeds germinate and plants grow the film is pushed upward and the slits open to allow air and water to pass in and out.

Whilst glass has been replaced by substitute materials in the larger structures, like the Festival Hall of the International Garden Festival in Liverpool, there has also been a boom in the use of much smaller structures like terrariums.

In 1829 a certain Dr Nathaniel Ward discovered, by accident, that green plants would thrive in sealed glass containers. The water transpired by plants and evaporated by soil condenses on the side of the glass and returns to the soil to be recycled again. Unless diseases

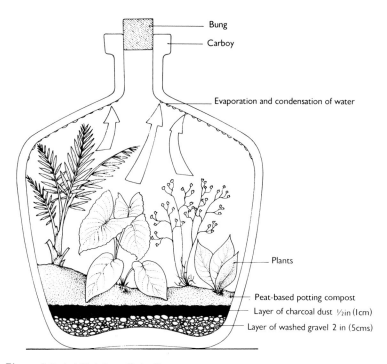

Figure 8.3 A Miniature Rain Forest

are already present they will be excluded and the recycling water prevents desiccation.

By the 1900s the Wardian case declined in popularity but in the 1980s the tradition has been revised in the form of terraria. The hot arid environment of the modern home or office block is unsuitable for most plants so container culture is the answer.

Terraria may take the form of aquaria or bottle gardens (Figure 8.3). The key thing is that once they are planted up they are kept air-tight by use of a lid or stopper. If the vessel remains 'steamed-up' the lid can be removed and replaced after a few minutes. After that the container should need little, if any, water. Avoid waterlogging at all costs and always choose plants that like humidity and are slow growing.

The use of protective structures has led to a greatly increased range of plants available to the gardener. This in turn has stimulated a massive demand for plants. More and more choice specimens are requested and only effective multiplication of them can satisfy this demand. It is to this subject, propagation, that we shall turn now.

9 The Secret of Immortality?

MARY ANN'S APPLE

In 1805, the year of the Battle of Trafalgar, Mary Ann Brailsford ate an apple. Not a cause for celebration you might think, but she sowed one of the pips from the core in her mother's cottage garden, at Southwell in Nottinghamshire, and it grew to fruit. Not only did it fruit well but the crop was so good for cooking that nurserymen in the area took shoots for grafting. It was eventually named after the new owner of the garden, a Mr Bramley. So the Bramley's Seedling apple came into being.

Although many people know about propagation, the multiplying of plants by sowing seeds, there are many other methods available – and people find grafting the most mysterious. But why not use seeds all the time?

Seeds are the product of pollen and eggs taken from two separate plants. Even if a carefully managed breeding programme has been followed there is no guarantee that all the offspring will be identical, just like the sons or daughters of a family would not be expected to be alike in every respect. Secondly if large plants like shrubs and trees are required it would take many years to grow them from seed, in some cases longer than any one gardener's lifetime.

Thirdly sometimes the genetic make-up changes spontaneously, a variegated stem or leaf may be produced on an otherwise uniformly green plant for example, and to try to continue this characteristic by using seed would be useless. Some kind of cutting is needed instead. Lastly, vegetative propagation is a good way of quickly producing disease-free stock.

OFFSETS AND PLANTLETS

Increasing stock without relying on flowers and their seeds is nothing new. This vegetative propagation is carried out naturally in many ways, without the intervention of gardeners, and none more commonly than the offset.

Offsets are young plants produced alongside the parent and are easily separated from it. Strictly speaking offsets are the offspring of bulbs, like daffodils, corms, like *Crocus*, and rosette-making plants including *Sempervivum* (houseleeks) and the bromeliads. These offsets all have sufficient roots to pot-on directly and given time and tender, loving care will grow as big as their parents.

The word 'offset' is also applied to the branches of cacti and succulents which, once detached, may also produce adventitious roots as an aid to becoming healthy independent plants. The key thing here is not the name but the fact that all the offshoots will be identical to the parent.

Some 'Tom Thumbs' of the gardener's world are worth a closer examination. *Bryophyllum daigremontianum*, the Mother of Thousands, and *Tolmiea menziesii*, the Pick-a-Back plant, produce miniature replicas of themselves. In the former case little plantlets are produced around the margins of the leaf, they fall off with the least vibration – even a harsh word from a passer-by will often do it – and they root without difficulty. *Tolmeia* plantlets, on the other hand, need to touch moist bare earth before rooting occurs. The production of plantlets is widespread, even in the 'monocots' like lilies, onions and grasses smaller versions of the parents are often to be found clinging to the shoots or flowers.

Other natural methods of propagation have been previously covered (Chapter 3) and have been used extensively by people but the human race has not been slow to exploit other methods too.

PROPAGATION BY CUTTINGS

Cuttings have been used by many generations of people in order to confer immortality on prize plant specimens. They can be portions of leaves, stems or roots – whatever works best – which are treated so as to produce roots and thus survive independently.

A whole range of specimens can be propagated using their leaves including; *Begonia, Crassula, Echeveria, Gloxinia, Peperomia, Saintpaulia, Sansevieria* and *Streptocarpus*.

The same applies to stem cuttings which are usually classified as softwood, semi-ripe or ripe (hardwood) cuttings. Softwood cuttings are made from immature tips which have no woody tissues. These include *Chrysanthemum, Pelargonium* and *Impatiens*. Semi-ripe cuttings are taken from the mature shoots of woody plants including deciduous and evergreen shrubs, heathers and conifers.

Ripe (hardwood) cuttings are made from the mature – brown – shoots of any woody plant. These are the easiest as they often have no need of extra heat and so can be readily used in the open. Many experts take 'heeled' cuttings. That is, they pull suitable cuttings downward so that a small piece of the main branch is torn off too. This 'heel' is trimmed to prevent any rotting. Stem cuttings are usually taken just below a node (leaf joint), as in *Pelargonium*, but others prefer to be internodal rather than nodal, like *Clematis*.

All cuttings rely on having enough auxin hormone within themselves to stimulate the formation of roots at their base. They should not be too small otherwise they exhaust their food reserves before the roots are made. They also need plenty of light, warmth and moisture so that they can grow quickly.

Within the base of the cutting the cambial cells (see Figures 4.4 and 4.5) divide to produce adventitious roots and more tissues for the developing plant. If a 'heeled cutting' is required a sliver of bark is removed along with the cutting. This exposes more cambial tissue ready for rooting.

Strangely, some plants are best propagated by using much smaller parts. For example *Dieffenbachia*, grape vines, *Dracaena*, *Wisteria* and *Camellia* can be increased using 'eye' cuttings – a short length of ripened stem containing a single growth bud (at the node). It is even possible to use an eye cutting which possesses a leaf, a so-called leaf bud cutting, which would help to feed the developing plant. This works very well with *Camellia japonica*.

No matter whether cuttings are taken from stems or leaves they must be protected from drying out. At the simplest level this can be achieved by covering the plants with a polythene bag and moving them out of direct sunlight. The most advanced mist propagation units achieve the same effect by delivering fine sprays at regular intervals. Often the switch for the mist-sprayer is operated by an 'electronic leaf'. Basically this is a system which is switched off by water spread across the 'leaf' but as soon as evaporation has removed this film of water, along with the water from the cuttings, the switch is turned on.

Plants which have thick tap roots can be propagated using just short sections of root. *Acanthus, Anchusa, Althea rosea* (Hollyhock), perennial *Limonium, Papaver orientalis* (oriental poppy), *Verbascum* (Mullein) and even horseradish (*Cochlearia armoracia*). A few fibrous-rooted plants can also be propagated in this way like *Phlox* and *Gaillardia*. It is vital to the former as it can produce eelworm-free stock. Fortunately this pest does not enter the *Phlox* roots.

PROPAGATION BY GRAFTING

Long before the secrets of inheritance had been revealed by Mendel, grafting had been used. Grafting was used by Chinese and Romans many centuries ago and was an art form in Europe by the eighteenth century when the Bramley's Seedling appeared.

It should not be forgotten that grafting can occur in Nature. Branches and roots which rub against one another can, if conditions are correct, unite. When the wounded tissue expands it is the cambial tissue which multiplies to produce callus cells. Eventually the two plants will grow as one, exchanging water and foods as they develop.

Grafting is ideal for raising plants which are difficult to raise by cuttings or for some reason cannot satisfactorily be grown using their own, natural roots or perhaps cannot be grown true from seed.

Apples and pears are not grown on their roots for several reasons. Firstly they sometimes make large trees with little fruit. Secondly they often will not root easily. Thirdly they are prone to root troubles.

Just as the foundations of a building are vital to the overall outcome of a design and are regularly forgotten, so are the roots of the tree, which determine the eventual size of the specimen. Not only this, but roots will decide how long it will be before the tree fruits, how much fruit it will carry and whether the tree will need support.

The ultimate height of an apple tree may be anything from 4 ft (1.3 m) to 18 ft (6 m) depending on the rootstock used (Figure 9.1 and Table 9.1). Similarly pears, quinces, medlars, cherries, plums, peaches, nectarines and apricots may be made to reach a predetermined height just by using the right rootstock. It is always best to use virus-free rooting material. In Britain the East Malling Research Station, Kent has done more than any other to provide disease-free rootstock with predictable characteristics.

It takes two to make a marriage and this marriage of plant parts would not be complete without compatible shoot material. The shoot or scion is selected for its fruiting characteristics. Whether it produces Cox's

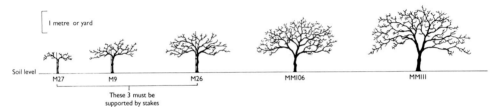

Figure 9.1 Ten Years' Growth of Different Rootstocks

Orange Pippin or American Red apples is decided by the scion.

In Britain, Long Ashton Research Station is foremost in producing virus-free shoots for grafting. EMLA material is commonly advertised – this is a product of East Malling rootstock and Long Ashton scion material. In the United States, similar schemes operate to ensure production of virus-free materials.

Scions are bound in place by raffia, plastic tape or any other material that will allow expansion as the plant grows. Usually grafting wax covers the binding material so that no infection can enter and the wound is not allowed to dry out.

There are as many grafting methods as there are

Table 9.1 How Tall Do You Want Your Fruit Trees?

Fruit	Rootstock	Approximate Eventual Height	
		ft	m
Apples	M27	4	1.30
	M26	8	2.50
	MM106	12	3.75
	M25	16	5.00
Pears	Quince 'C'	12	3.75
	Quince 'A'	16	5.00
Cherry	Colt	16	5.00
	F12.1	36	11.00
Plum	Pixy	12	3.75
Peach	St Julian 'A'	12	3.75
Nectarine	Mussell	16	5.00
Apricot	Brompton	18	6.00

Note: There are many other rootstocks available from specialist nurseries.

counties in Britain or States in North America. Indeed, this is the key because each locality found its own successful method and tended not to change. There are bottle grafts, bridge grafts, saddle grafts, side grafts, crown (rind) grafts, cleft grafts, whip (splice) grafts, stub grafts and tongue grafts but perhaps the most widely used today is the whip and tongue graft. This can be used for woody ornamental plants as well as fruit trees.

Using a very sharp knife, the rootstock should be cut downwards starting 6 in (15 cm) above the soil (Figure 9.2). The line of the cut should be a zigzag one. The scion should be cut so as to match the cut of the rootstock. When placed together no light should be seen between the two. This is bound and hot wax used to seal the union.

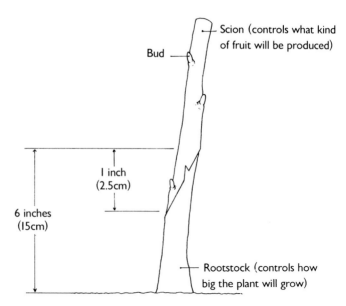

Figure 9.2 Graft Your Own Tree

Some rootstock and scion materials are incompatible so 'double-working' is used. For example, the pear cultivars 'Packham's Triumph', 'William's Bon Chretien', 'Dr Jules Guyot' and 'Bristol' cross are not compatible when worked onto quince rootstock so if such a graft is required, a piece of the cultivar 'Beurre Hardy' is used as bridging tissue.

Once a successful grafting method had been achieved then experiments began to see how many cultivars could be raised on a single rootstock. No one knows what the record is but commonly up to six cultivars are used on a 'family apple' tree. This has great advantages for the gardener with a small garden. For example, 'James Grieve', 'Golden Delicious' and 'Laxton Superb' can give eating apples from September through to December. Pears can be made to do likewise. By using a dwarfing rootstock an 'orchard' can be raised in nothing more than a row of large tubs.

Fruit trees are not the only plants to be grafted – cacti, ornamental trees like cherries and most roses all depend on this process. Cacti are the easiest because after cutting two plants, one is placed on another and pinned.

With all grafted plants growth from the rootstock, called 'suckers', must be removed or it will take the lion's share of the food supply and will grow at the expense of the scion. The best remedy is to remove them, usually by pulling them off, where they join the roots. If they are chopped off at soil level more suckers will grow so treatment must be at the source of the problem and not just where they emerge from the soil.

CELL MANIPULATION

It was as early as 1838 that two Germans by the name of Schleiden and Schwann first turned their thoughts to what plant cells might be capable of.

By 1902 another German called Haberlandt took up the idea of culturing plant cells but it was 20 years later that the tips of grass shoots were isolated and persuaded to grow root systems. Unfortunately they died shortly afterwards. By 1934 tomato roots were grown. Later leaves and other plant parts were used. All that they needed was water, sugar, vitamins, minerals salts and the correct temperature.

This was not just a novelty, it had practical value. For example, virus-free material could be grown to increase the quality and yield of crops. Also this could prove of use for plants which do not breed true to type from seed or perhaps are sterile and incapable of seed production.

Another approach was tried. Wound or callus material was cultured along with hormones in order to bring about development of roots and shoots. During this work some previously known plant diseases were recognised as being due to hormone imbalance. There was crown gall on the stem of *Petunia hybrida* for example which was caused by *Agrobacterium tumefaciens*. This bacterium upset the host plant hormones so much that the gall or swelling appeared.

Other diseases we found to be caused by other things. Leafhopper insects (*Aureogenus magnivena*) were discovered to carry a virus which produced wound tumour disease.

It may seem staggering but since 1956 it has been possible to keep single plant cells, like those extracted from the French bean (*Phaseolus vulgaris*), dividing continuously – although only in test-tubes. Later leaf cells of the plume poppy (*Macleaya cordata*), the snapdragon (*Antirrhinum majus*), *Datura innoxia* and the tobaccos (*Nicotiana tabacum* and *N. sylvestris*) followed suit.

A breakthrough came in 1970 when single tobacco leaf cells were made to produce little plantlets. Think of the consequences. It is now possible to bring into existence new, artificially-produced plants or modify existing ones. By using chemicals like EMS (ethyl methane-sulphonate) or irradiations, like X-rays, ultra-violet light and gamma rays, it is possible to bring about mutations. In other words increased variation can be deliberately brought about. Flower colour and number, size and shape of foliage and so on can be introduced and the best offspring selected. Orange (*Citrus sinensis*) has already been treated in this way.

The single cells found within pollen grains of one plant and the eggs of another otherwise incompatible plant can be fused to create a new species. This really is exciting stuff.

The best is yet to come, though. Since we know that the key to what cells can do is tied up in the genes they contain it should eventually be possible to introduce beneficial genes into selected cells and then grow these cells into individual plants. Every farmer's dream is to not have to pay bills for fertilisers. If the bacterial genes that make plant foods, like nitrates, could be introduced into plant cells there will be no need for fertilisers.

Rather than use a single cell others have made great strides using shoot tips. The progress using the carnation (*Dianthus* species) has been dramatic. First the 'patients' are kept at 100°F (38°C) at 85-90 per cent relative humidity for two months then the shoot tips are chopped off and when the 'test tube technicians' have made sure that they have developed the carnation roots and leaves the plantlets are potted up in the greenhouse conditions, free of viruses and insect pests.

Orchids too have benefited. Usually they are popular houseplants and cut flowers but they are very expensive. Alas, their seeds are difficult if not impossible to germinate by conventional means and therefore seeds were germinated on special sterile culture before transfer to potting mixtures. Unfortunately, although this method

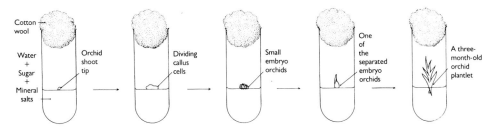

Figure 9.3 How to Clone an Orchid

works the seedlings take many years to mature and many are then discarded because of their poor quality of flowers.

The breakthrough came in 1960 when the shoot tips of *Cymbidium* orchids were encouraged to produce little embryos (Figure 9.3). Embryos are divided up so that each piece can develop into a separate plant each of which will be identical to the others in every respect, these are called clones. This method was extended to other orchids like *Cattleya* so their price could be reduced.

Similar techniques have now been used for gooseberries (*Ribes uva-crispa*), hop (*Humulus lupulus*), potato (*Solanum tuberosum*) and rhubarb (*Rheum* × *ananassa*). Unfortunately, some offspring still contain viruses so they have to be rigorously tested by taking an extract, painting this on host plants and watching to see if they become infected.

There really is no limit to the ingenuity of people. The plants of the future will no doubt include most of those that we see about us now but many will be new and of very different form from those available at present. One problem that will still arise is that of pest and disease control and that is the next topic in our scientific study.

10 Are All Gardeners Trouble-makers?

ASKING FOR TROUBLE

It is easy to imagine that the garden is a place of perfect peace and harmony where everything is in balance, but nothing could be further from the truth. Gardens are battlegrounds, or at least they should be if gardeners are doing their jobs properly.

The problem is this: in the wild there is a state of equilibrium where no animal or plant gains greatly in numbers because as they increase so do the predators that feed upon them. Equally, when their numbers decrease the predators fall in number too so there are always control mechanisms to make sure nothing gets out of hand.

In the garden it is a different story. If a lawn is a success it is composed of grass and nothing else, a so-called monoculture. In the flower beds it is the same story. Often bedding plants are arranged in great numbers without variety.

Such monocultures are very prone to attack from all manner of pests and diseases. Lawns may be troubled by toadstools and lichens, excavated by earthworms, mined by moles and attacked by ants. Flowers are prone to attack by 'worms' and weevils, rots and moulds, thrips and bugs.

If gardeners will persist in growing large numbers of the same plant very close together, be it fruit, vegetables or flowers, then war must be declared. By growing mixtures of specimens, some gardeners have found that the odd cabbage in amongst the ornamental plants works well enough, the problem can be reduced but rarely eradicated. Chemicals need to be used.

CATEGORIES OF PESTICIDES

Pests are all forms of animal life which cause damage to

plants. Pesticides have been devised to combat pests and they can be subdivided depending on what they kill (Table 10.1). Insecticides kill all insects, six-legged creatures with a body divided into three parts (head, thorax and abdomen) and two antennae ('feelers'), whether they be flies, beetles or bees. Note the last example, if sprayed indiscriminately insecticides will kill beneficial insects like pollinating bees, as well as hated adversaries like aphids.

Other pesticides include molluscides which destroy any mollusc like slugs and snails. Then there are acaricides which kill arachnids like the fruit tree scourge called red spider mite. Other, less used pesticides are ovicides which kill eggs, particularly those of insects like butterflies and moths. Finally, there are nematocides which eliminate eelworms.

If plants are not troubled by pests then diseases may be the problem. Fungi, bacteria and viruses also attack plants but sometimes specimens suffer from a lack of certain foods and a deficiency disease occurs.

So fungicides (Table 10.2) and bactericides (antibiotics) have been devised to combat these. Benomyl fungicide is exceptional because it enters the plant tissues and when fungi begin to invade the plant the fungicide kills them on contact. In other words it is a systemic fungicide. Viruses cannot be successfuly dealt with by amateur gardeners and any plants suffering from virus diseases should be destroyed. Deficiency diseases are best solved by applying a balanced feed.

HOW SAFE ARE GARDEN CHEMICALS?

It is right that people should be anxious about all the manufactured chemicals that are added to gardens these days but they are only available today after many years of investigation and experimentation. Every new chemical to come on to the market has been selected from thousands of possible candidates over a period of up to ten years and costing anything up to £15,000,000. This massive expenditure will have meant research in laboratories and greenhouses backed up by tests on experimental garden plots. If a chemical passes all these tests it is then subjected to large-scale field trials for several seasons in a wide variety of local conditions.

All garden chemicals must satisfy a number of key requirements. They must effectively do their job, be it controlling a pest or disease, be cheap enough for

Table 10.1 Which Pesticide?

Active Ingredient (brand names vary)	Systemic?	Mites	Aphides	Caterpillars	Beetles	Ants	Soil pests	Scale insects	Comments
Biomesrethrin		✓	✓	✓					Very effective against whitefly.
Borax						✓			
Bromophos					✓	✓	✓		Useful at end of pest dormant season.
Butoxicarboxim	✓	✓	✓					✓	Used in plant 'pins'.
Carbaryl				✓	✓	✓	✓		Harms some plants.
Chlorbenside		✓							
+ Chlorbenzilate		✓							
+ Chlorobenzoate		✓							
Chlordane						✓			Also against earthworms.
Chlorpyrifos							✓		
Demeton		✓	✓						
Demeton-S-methyl		✓	✓						
Diazinon							✓		
Dichlorvos (DDVP)		✓	✓					✓	Against stem borers.
Dicofol		✓							
Dimethoate	✓		✓	✓				✓	Against stem borers.
gamma-HCH (Lindane)			✓	✓			✓	✓	Against stem borers.
Malathion		✓	✓	✓		✓	✓	✓	Also stem borers. Harms fish.
Metaldehyde							✓		Snails, slugs and millipedes too.
Nicotine			✓	✓					Also stem borers.
Oxydemeton-methyl		✓	✓	✓					Usually an aerosol.
Permethrin			✓	✓					
Petroleum oil						✓		✓	
Perimicarb			✓						
Pyrethrum			✓	✓	✓				
Resmethrin		✓	✓	✓	✓				
Rotenone (Derris)		✓	✓	✓					
Tar oil			✓	✓				✓	
Trichlorphon				✓	✓				Also stem borers.

Note: Many others are available.

Table 10.2 Which Fungicide?

Active Ingredient (brand names vary)	Systemic?	Diseases
Benomyl	✓	Wide-ranging, including club root and as a preventive measure for bulbs, etc.
Bordeaux Mixture (copper sulphate + lime)		Wide-ranging, including fruit tree scab and potato blight. Harms fish.
Cheshunt Compound (copper sulphate + ammonium carbonate)		Especially to prevent damping off of seedlings.
Dichlofluanid		Wide-ranging, including strawberry botrytis, tulip fire and rose black spot.
Dinocap (Karathane)		Powdery mildews. Not to be inhaled or left on skin. Can harm fish.
Folpet		Many diseases, including mildew and rose black spot.
Mancozeb		Wide-ranging, including lawn diseases and rusts.
Maneb		Wide-ranging, including downy mildews and rose black spot. Not to be inhaled.
Mercurous chloride (Calomel		Onion white rot, club root and lawn diseases.
Quintozene		Bulb diseases, root rots and lawn diseases.
Sulphur		Storage rots and powdery mildew.
Tecnazene (TCNB)		Fumigant. Grey mould.
Thiram		Wide-ranging. Mildews, rusts, lawn diseases, damping off and animal repellent. Can taint produce and irritate skin.

Table 10.2 cont.

Active Ingredient (brand names vary)	Systemic?	Diseases
Zineb		Wide-ranging. Not to be inhaled or left on skin.

Notes: 1. Notice how few systemic fungicides there are.
2. Many others are available.

gardeners to buy, be easy to apply and, most important, be safe to use.

A detailed programme of toxicological testing examines any immediate or long-term effects of the pesticide on animals and plants apart from those being treated. Rats, mice, birds, bees, fish and eventually human volunteers are all used to make sure that they do not suffer from the chemical. Up to 15 per cent of the total costs may be spent on this aspect of development.

In addition the chemical industry takes very seriously its duty not only to offer safe products but also to provide adequate labels. For example new symbols introduced by the EEC Council of Europe and voluntarily adopted by pesticide producers provide information on the hazards of garden chemicals (Figure 10.1).

Toxic

Oxidising

Harmful or irritant

Corrosive

Explosive

Flammable

Figure 10.1 Learn Your Labels

In the United Kingdom, pesticide producers and the government work together. The Agricultural Chemicals Approval scheme, operated by the Ministry of Agriculture, Fisheries and Food, gives approval to the new product providing it is satisfied it will do the job for which it will be recommended. Where the letter 'A' appears before the proprietary name it indicates that it has been given official approval.

In the United States, similar precautions exist and come under a Code of Federal Regulations. The Environmental Protection Agency plays a major role in ensuring the safety of pesticides (401 M Street, South West, Washington, DC 20460).

Under the Pesticides Safety Precautions Scheme the toxicological research and other information relating to the safety of the chemical is submitted to an Advisory Committee and after full consideration it recommends any precautions that are to be taken when the product is used. They name the crops to which it can be applied and the interval that must elapse between the final treatment and harvest. All these precautions must be stated on the labels of packs containing the pesticide.

Some pesticides are therefore marked as harmful to certain plants. For example gamma-HCH (BHC or lindane) is harmful to cucumbers, marrows, melons, hydrangeas, young tomatoes and vines. To avoid possible tainted produce this insecticide should also not be used on fruit and vegetables near harvest-time or as a seed dressing (a protective coat for seeds) on onion, leek, lettuce or radish seeds.

Dimethoate insecticide should never be used on *Calceolaria*, ornamental *Prunus*, *Cineraria* and *Chrysanthemum*. No pesticides containing sulphur should be sprayed on apples, pears, plums, gooseberries or currants. Finally malathion insecticide has been known to harm the flowers and foliage of *Fuchsia*, ferns, *Crassula*, *Gerbera*, *Pilea*, *Zinnia*, *Petunia*, *Antirrhinum* and sweet peas. It pays to read the label! If the label does not specify the contents and their proper use do not use the product.

Some gardeners worry about garden chemicals upsetting the Balance of Nature but, of course, it is true that gardens are no more natural than large fields of cereals or fruit orchards. However, it has been discovered that residues do remain in the environment long after use of the chemical. The argument runs that such residues are extremely small and there is no evidence of any long-term effects on people. Both of these statements are true but it is a matter of concern to everyone that 'left overs' of garden chemicals do remain. Certainly it is not a matter for complacency and all gardeners should be aware of their responsibility when applying chemicals and only do so safely, according to the manufacturer's instructions and when absolutely necessary.

As a direct result of the concern of growers the persistent organochlorine insecticides, like DDT, have been actively discouraged, if not outlawed, particularly for edible crops. The organophosphorus insecticides, like malathion, which break down rapidly on application or the non-toxic chemicals, like rotenone (derris) and pyrethrum, are suitable alternatives.

TYPES OF PESTICIDE

Pesticides can be applied in a multiplicity of ways: as liquids (where the chemical goes into solution), emulsions (here the chemical is dispersed in the liquid but is too big to become dissolved), wettable powders (these are made into a paste and then mixed with water), aerosols (a very fine spray of droplets or dust particles), dusts (dry powders usually applied by a 'puffer'), smokes and fumigates (fine particles carried by convection currents from a hot smoke generator in a confined space like a greenhouse) and 'spikes' or 'pins' (which are solid lengths of pesticide-impregnated material to be pushed into potting mixtures).

Pesticides, and for that matter fungicides too, work in a variety of ways. Some work as contact poisons. When insects or fungi touch the poison they die within a very short time. Such garden chemicals are metabolic poisons. That is, they upset the metabolism or internal chemistry of the pest or disease and because it cannot function properly it dies.

Other pesticides are stomach poisons. These kill any small animal feeding on the vegetation. Systemic compounds are stomach poisons too but work in a unique way. These chemicals are absorbed through the stomata on the leaves, pass into the sap circulating in the phloem and are transported to all parts of the plant. When sap-sucking insects, like aphids or mites like red spider mite, insert their mouthparts into the phloem to feed they drink the fatal brew and die.

Pesticides need to be used frequently. Any residue left on foliage will be washed off by any water, from rain or otherwise, and some are broken down so quickly that they cannot be expected to be effective for more than a few days. Sometimes they are referred to as 'knock down' chemicals because that is just what they do to offending pests and diseases. The great advantage of systemic insecticides is that they will continue circulating within the plant sap and offer their protective qualities for several weeks. It is always best to mix pesticides with a few drops of washing-up liquid in order to make sure that the plant becomes well wetted with the spray, as it breaks down the surface tension of the water and lets it run freely over the foliage.

PLAY IT SAFE

Just when the garden looks a picture and you smack your lips with expectation as you dream of the fruit and vegetables about to come to the dining table, disaster strikes, at least it seem to be that way for many gardeners.

Most gardeners reach for the poison bottle when animal pests and plant diseases annihilate their precious garden plants – to kill the pests not themselves! – however, by following six basic guidelines many pests and diseases can be avoided.

1. Play it safe by making sure your soil is pest-free and fertile. Remove as many animals as you can from your plot as you cultivate it and leave only the earthworm. By digging, rotating crops and liming, if necessary, on a regular basis you will lessen the chance of fungal disease like club root (a fungal infection of *Cruciferae* like cabbages) and pests like woodlice and wireworms (the young of beetles often called click beetles or skipjacks).

2. Ensure that any seeds, bulbs and plants you use are of the highest quality. Whenever possible use resistant or immune cultivars to guard against diseases known to be prevalent in your area; the F_1 cultivars are particularly useful here. With soft fruit like strawberries and potatoes likewise buy certified virus-free stock. A look over the garden fence into your neighbour's garden will tell you at a glance which flowers, fruits, vegetables and ornamental plants do well, or otherwise, in your locality.

3. Make sure you follow planting instructions to the letter especially taking note of the timing, depth and spacing required for each type. Stake plants if required.

4. Provide enough foods for the plants. A lack of NPK or any of the other nutrients will render the plants less resistant to attacks by pests and diseases. In fact, for most specimens, application of a base dressing like bone meal when planting and a top dressing high in potash

during the growing season usually provides all the plant foods needed.

5. Give freshly planted specimens plenty to drink. Established plants need water only when signs of wilting are seen, over-watering can lead to infection by pests and diseases.

6. Always remove garden rubbish, dead plants and weeds to reduce the breeding ground for the gardener's adversaries.

APHIDS

Life on safari is full of the excitement of seeing the big game but your own garden can be a great source of interest too. Take the blackfly and greenfly for example.

These aphids, or plant leeches or lice as they are sometimes called, seem to live in depressingly large numbers on roses and runner beans. All these insects have the same soft oval bodies, small heads, compound (multifaceted) eyes, antennae and a sharp proboscis ('beak') for piercing the plant to feed from the sap. Usually these disease-ridden vampires are about $1/_{10}$ in (2 mm) long and produce such sweet waste products that sooty moulds grow on them and disfigure the plant.

The life cycle of an aphid is bizarre. After mating in the summer and autumn eggs are laid on trees. These hatch the following spring as winged females which fly or are carried up to hundreds of miles at great altitudes to reach food plants in new territories.

A single mother may produce up to 25 daughters a day which can themselves breed after only eight days. If all the offspring of a mother lived and reproduced throughout a single year their combined weight would be equal to 500,000,000 gardeners. At the end of the summer winged females return to the original kind of host plant to lay eggs which hatch into both sexes and the cycle begins again.

FRIENDS OF THE GARDENER

Fortunately for the amateur gardener the plant leech has many enemies including birds, spiders, mites and the ladybirds. A safari is never complete until a beautiful bird has been spotted. The ladybird is the garden version of the Bird of Paradise.

They are small brightly-coloured beetles which represent the end of a life cycle lasting four to seven weeks. Up to 200 eggs are laid on the underside of leaves near aphids and these hatch after a week into small, lively, bristly grubs coloured black, orange, blue and red. It is this stage which is most beneficial for gardeners since a single larva will eat several hundred aphids in three weeks. In parts of the world where aphids are a problem, as in California, ladybirds are sometimes introduced by the tens of millions to do the job they do best, as aphid annihilators.

It is important to remember that ladybirds and all insects will be killed by any insecticide with which they come into contact. Open flowers should never be sprayed because of the danger of killing pollinating insects like bees.

Other forms of biological control, or integrated post management as it is sometimes known, can be deliberately introduced by gardeners. Only three are of especial interest today. In greenhouses eggs of the 'wasp' *Encarsia formosa* can be hatched to release insects which attack whitefly. However, once the pest has been eliminated the wasp numbers drop and unfortunately this means that if another outbreak occurs the wasp will have to be reintroduced again and again. This could prove a costly process.

Secondly, the spores of bacteria (*Bacillus thuringiensis* and *Bacillus popilliae*) can be sprayed on to crops attacked by caterpillars and Japanese beetle grubs respectively. The spores hatch into bacteria which are eaten by the pest and produce proteins poisonous to the pest and eliminate them.

Thirdly, the dreaded red spider mite can be removed from glasshouses by introducing another mite called *Phytoseiulus* which can eat up to five adults or 20 young pests every day. Again, like the Brazilian *Encarsia*, the Chilean mite cannot stand low winter temperatures and so needs to be introduced every season.

Many gardeners have found that using certain flowers helps to ward off certain pests. Take Marigolds (*Tagetes*) for example. When planted between tomatoes and cucumbers in the greenhouse these not only provide an ornamental feature but naturally produce insecticide in their flowers which keeps the whitefly at bay, at least that is the theory.

VIRUSES

When something nasty strikes your garden plants and it does not crawl, and therefore cannot be an animal pest, or appear as a growth over the shoots and leaves, and therefore cannot be a plant disease, the chances are that a virus is implicated.

The tell-tale signs of viroid attack are usually seen in the leaves. Such infected leaves may become completely yellow or just lose their green pigment (chlorophyll) in patches to create a mosaic pattern. Often associated with loss of colour is a crinkling or distortion of the leaves. Additionally leaves may become white-veined and stems striped.

Viruses consist of a protein coat which acts like a space-shuttle to carry a cargo. Whereas the space-shuttle carries satellites and experiments the virus carries genetic material which joins that within the plant cells in order to make more of itself. Insects, eelworms, birds and mites often carry viruses, aphids do so frequently but people can easily transfer them with their fingers too. Tobacco mosaic virus for example has been spread by many a smoker.

Virus-diseased plants cannot be controlled by chemicals and are best lifted and destroyed but make sure you wash your hands afterwards and keep control of the pests that may carry the disease.

Fortunately viruses are not all bad news, though. In some ornamental plants like tulips and wallflowers 'flower-breaking' occurs which means that light coloured, often white or yellow, streaks develop on otherwise dark coloured petals. The effects of viruses on leaves can be very valuable and dramatic too. *Abutilon striatum* 'Thompsonii' has leaves heavily mottled with yellow and is deliberately perpetuated because of this character.

Table 10.3 Golden Rules for Using Pesticides

1. *Choose the right product.* Decide whether you need an insecticide or fungicide and if so, what type.
2. *Carefully read the manufacturer's instructions* and stick to them.
3. *Avoid drifting* of your chemicals on to other plants.
4. *Wash away any accidental spillage* immediately, using copious amounts of water.
5. *After spraying, close tightly any partially full containers* and store them safely away from children and pets. *Never* store spray solution – make up fresh solution each time.
6. *Never transfer pesticides into other storage containers,* especially beer and lemonade bottles.
7. *Never mix chemicals* unless the manufacturer's instructions specify that it can be done.
8. *Wash your hands* very carefully after using pesticides. Many

people have been fatally poisoned because they forgot this
– the simplest of the rules.

9. *With persistent pesticides*, leave at least two weeks between
spraying and harvesting of edible crops. With non-
persistent pesticides only two days need to be left – but
always check the label.

10. *Change chemicals regularly* to prevent pests and diseases
becoming immune to attack.

11. *If someone has been poisoned* with pesticides, call a doctor
immediately, always give the name of the chemical(s) and
as much information as you can find out.

Whatever ails your plants make sure that you act like a
good doctor. First get your diagnosis correct. Check
every part of the stricken plants: the roots, stems, leaves,
flowers and fruits. If animals are suspected, find them.
Then, and only then, act and do so safely (Table 10.3).

Certain techniques that gardeners carry out are taken
for granted without necessarily trying to explain them. It
is to these that we shall turn next.

11 I Hoe, I Hoe . . .

TO HOE OR NOT TO HOE

Next time you pick up your hoe consider this. Over 2,000 years ago the Greeks used hoes, the Romans followed suit and in many parts of the world the same digging hoe is still the basic tool.

There is no doubt about it, the hoe is a vital tool in the gardener's arsenal. Not only will it till the soil, that is loosen the surface, but it will chop weeds off at ground level, make seed drills, pull and push earth around plants and perform a whole host of other jobs besides.

The spade first appeared in Roman times and complemented the hoe in that it could perform other jobs. Spades cultivate to much greater depths and rely on a lever system rather than just brute strength.

Levers rely on having a centre of balance (or fulcrum) and a weight at both ends. By applying pressure at one end a weight of soil can be moved at the other end. In order to make things easier, the longer the handle the easier the work is.

When you pick up the spadeful of soil the place where you hold the shaft of the spade becomes the fulcrum or pivot. The nearer the hand moves towards the blade, the easier it will be to push down the handle and lift up the soil. Unfortunately, the total weight of the soil is not changed and backache is still possible after excessive digging. The recent introduction of the 'automatic' spade which uses a spring to push the soil out of the earth is faster than an orthodox spade and certainly reduces backache problems.

Digging is one of the most common practices in all but the smallest plot but why do we do it? Since plants need air and water near the roots and no weeds nearby the digging process achieves just this. The soil is broken into smaller particles which have air and water between them and the weeds are buried. By following with a hoe and then a rake a 'fine tilth' can be obtained which, because the soil crumbs are so small, is ideal for seed germination and plant growth.

SINGLE DIGGING, DOUBLE DIGGING AND NO-DIGGING

Single digging is commonly used on regularly cultivated land. It is most efficient when, using the foot, the spade is driven vertically into the ground and then the spade is pulled back using the handle. Then the spade should be turned quickly to bury weeds completely.

Ideally it is best to excavate a trench at one end of the plot and carry the soil to the far end. If there is any manure or compost available then this should be spread on the whole soil surface and then the next strip is excavated, turned over and placed in the first trench so that any composted material becomes buried along with the vegetation.

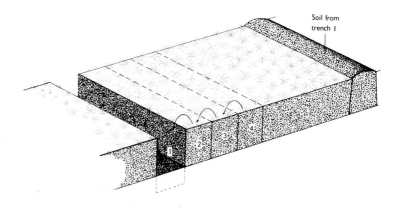

Soil from trench 1

Figure 11.1 Double Digging
A. *A trench one-spit deep is excavated and the soil placed in a heap at the other end of the plot to be dug.*
B. *The bottom of the trench (1) is forked over and manure or similar material worked in along with bone meal.*
C. *The soil from zone 2 is inverted and placed in trench 1.*
D. *Processes B and C are repeated.*

The enthusiasts of digging often reserve their finest praise for 'double digging' (Figure 11.1). This begins in the same way as single digging but once a trench is excavated the bottom of it is forked over thoroughly and compost or manure plus bone meal is mixed in too. Then the next strip of ground is turned into this trench and the process continues. Such hard work does not need to be done every year but is advisable every three or four years on vegetable and flower plots and on any land which has not been previously cultivated. Because double digging is much more thorough than single digging the trenches need to be wider, about 2 ft (60 cm) rather than 1 ft (30 cm) respectively.

Clay soils benefit greatly from digging in the autumn since this process exposes large clods of earth that will be broken down by frosts, which expand the water in the clay as it freezes, pushing the clods apart. When you get a 'frost tilth' leave it undisturbed for at least a week to make sure the soil dries before use. Autumn is a good time for most digging anyhow since most land, like annual flower beds and vegetable plots, will be vacant at this time.

Soil should never be cultivated in wet or frozen or very dry conditions. If soil is wet enough to stick to your shoes it is too wet to cultivate. Any weight on the soil will cause it to 'pan'. That is at some level, it may be more than 1 ft (30 cm) down, the soil particles will be compacted and prevent drainage. Soil pans slow down plant growth and might even kill them. If soil is frozen or very dry it will fracture as it is dug and the soil structure will break down.

If it sounds like you might never be able to dig or cultivate your soil because it always seems to be too wet or too dry or frozen, do not despair. There are many 'no-diggers' amongst the gardening brethren who believe that since Nature does not till the soil then why should people. There certainly is some power to this argument but if non-digging is the answer then you must be sure to avoid treading on the plot whenever possible. This means that the garden needs to be divided into small areas separated by paths so that gardeners can tend their charges without treading on the soil.

REGULAR ROTATION

In the vegetable plot digging in the autumn is usually followed by sowing in the spring but no one group of vegetables should be grown in the same bed year after year. The only exceptions to this rule seem to be onions and runner beans which appear to benefit from being in the same area permanently. If they do so they still need to be cared for by using fertilisers and pesticides. This is especially important in permanent beds where the ideal conditions for a build-up of pests and diseases over the year may occur.

It is precisely because plant foods decrease as pests and diseases increase when a vegetable is grown in one spot year after year that crop rotation was devised

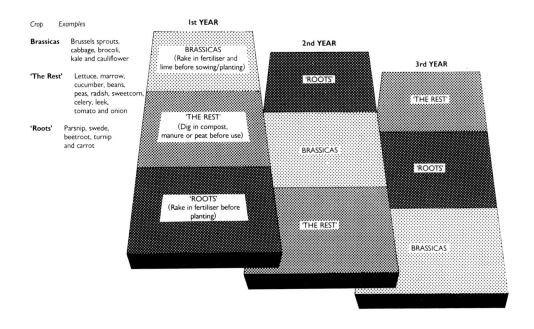

Crop	Examples
Brassicas	Brussels sprouts, cabbage, brocoli, kale and cauliflower
'The Rest'	Lettuce, marrow, cucumber, beans, peas, radish, sweetcorn, celery, leek, tomato and onion
'Roots'	Parsnip, swede, beetroot, turnip and carrot

1st YEAR

BRASSICAS
(Rake in fertiliser and lime before sowing/planting)

'THE REST'
(Dig in compost, manure or peat before use)

'ROOTS'
(Rake in fertiliser before planting)

2nd YEAR

'ROOTS'

BRASSICAS

'THE REST'

3rd YEAR

'THE REST'

'ROOTS'

BRASSICAS

Figure 11.2 A Three-year Vegetable Plot Rotation

(Figure 11.2). This basically means that the same crop does not occupy the same area in consecutive years.

Vegetables can be easily divided into three groups: *Brassicas*, 'roots' and 'the rest' (Figure 11.2). The plot is divided into three areas, one for each crop type. *Brassica* crops include cabbages, Brussels sprouts and cauliflower and all of these plants have two major requirements: nitrogen and lime. The nitrogen allows the leaves to grow and expand whereas the lime ensures that the pH of the soil is kept high enough, that is alkaline enough, to discourage the fungal disease club root as well as providing calcium for normal plant growth. If manure is used rather than artificial fertiliser then it should be applied at a different time to the lime otherwise the two will interact and do the garden no good.

'Roots' would include parsnips, carrots, potatoes, turnips, beetroots and swedes. All these need is a general fertiliser with phosphates so that root growth is encouraged. This would constitute the second part of the vegetable plot.

'The rest' would involve all vegetables that do not fall into the previous two categories. Crops like leeks, lettuces, radishes, peas, tomatoes, beans, celery, sweet corn and cucumbers could be cultivated in this patch of ground. In the autumn before planting compost, manure or peat should be dug into this area.

The following year each crop must move into another area. *Brassica* plants go into the zone previously occupied by 'the rest'. This is an important move. By using crops like peas and beans, which fix atmospheric nitrogen in a chemical form which plants can take up, the *Brassicas* that follow them are given a free supply of nitrogen. If root crops were put on this ground they would make far too much leaf growth and develop very poor roots.

Root crops are put on to the ground occupied before by *Brassicas*. This makes good sense too because the *Brassicas* will have used much of the available nitrogen and so the root crops will be encouraged to make root growth. Lastly, 'the rest' of the vegetable crops follow root crops and since they have no particular appetite for phosphates then they should do very well. This is a three-year rotation system. Other systems have been devised for two, four or five years and all of them try to capitalise on the fact that additions and depletions made by one crop can be beneficial to the next crop.

PRUNING

Another traditional practice often carried out without always realising the reasons for it, is pruning. This process can be applied to a whole range of plants, from herbaceous specimens like *Pelargonium* which often have their shoot tips pinched out to lopping whole branches from mature trees.

The reasons behind pruning are fourfold; first, to remove any damaged, dead or diseased material; secondly, to shape the plant according to the gardener's requirements; thirdly, to remove any plant parts not required so that the plant is kept within bounds; and, lastly, to encourage flower and fruit production.

Whole manuals have been written on fruit, ornamental, tree and bush pruning but several points are always borne in mind. Whatever tools are used, be it secateurs or saws, must be clean and sharp. Infection must be prevented at all costs and by not introducing pests on the blade and producing clean cuts this possibility is greatly reduced.

Also, how much material is to be cut away must be carefully considered. Generally the 'harder' the pruning, that is the more that is cut away, the more vigorous will be the resulting growth. What is more such growth will be from the buds nearest the cut. Such buds will have been kept dormant by the shoot tip which will have used the best of the foods, water and hormones for itself. This rapid growth will often be vegetative, that is it will produce shoots but few flowers and fruit.

A good example is *Eucalyptus* which can be regularly pruned hard back in order that it will produce its lovely juvenile foliage. Other ornamental shrubs like *Buddleia* (the butterfly bush) and *Salix* (willows) thrive after annual hard pruning.

'Light' pruning is reserved for fruit trees and any other plants that need keeping within bounds but bountiful in flower and fruit production. Critical in this respect is whether fruit is carried on 'old' or 'new' wood.

Alternatively rambler roses, black currants and raspberries all use year-old stems to flower and fruit best. For this reason the shoots which have performed their function are pruned out every year.

WEEDS – THE GARDENER'S COMMON ENEMY

Weeds – that dreaded word sticks in most gardeners' throats, because these very successful plants seem to occupy far too much time in the average garden. Weeds are plants growing in the wrong place, many of them are highly adapted to resist removal and in the past two methods have been used to remove them; cultivation and mulching.

Perhaps the two commonest cultivation techniques employed to eradicate weeds are digging and hoeing, the former to bury them and the latter to chop them off at ground level. Unfortunately the short-lived weeds tend to seed quickly so even though the mother plants have been buried the offspring are often already germinating. Similarly perennial weeds often use long tap roots so that removal of just the top of the plant does not kill them.

By using natural materials, like peat and compost, or artificial products, like black plastic, as a mulch on the ground around plants it has been possible to exclude that thing vital to all weed growth, light. Without light weeds wither but organic mulches need to be thick and regularly renewed whereas inorganic ones are not aesthetically pleasing.

What seems to be an insurmountable problem has sought the help of science and the answer came in the chemical form of herbicides or weed killers (Table 11.1). Herbicides must be used carefully since they are plant killers and indiscriminate use can ruin roses and *Clematis*,

Table 11.1 Which Herbicide?

Active Ingredient	Mode of Action	Uses
Aminotriazole	Total: Translocated	Uncultivated ground, paths, roads.
Ammonium sulphomate (AMS)	Total: Contact	Persistent weeds and tree stumps.
Chlorpropham (CIPC)	Selective	Against grass and weeds in young stages.
Copper sulphate	Selective	Broad-leaved weeds and water weeds.
2, 4-D	Selective: Translocated	Broad-leaved weeds, often on lawns.
Dalapon	Selective: Translocated	Grasses, e.g. couch, among trees, shrubs and in crops like potato.
Dicamba	Selective	Broad-leaved weeds. Can be leached to other plants. *Very persistent.
Dichlobenil	Total	*Very persistent. Can damage trees and shrubs.
Dichlorophen	Selective	Mosses, liverworts and algae on paths. Also kills fungi (toadstools) on lawns.
Diquat	Contact: Partial translocated	Annuals and perennials. Inactivated by soil.
Diuron	Total	Limited leaching in soil. *Very persistent.
Fenoprop	Growth regulator	Stops perennial weeds growing. *Very persistent.
Glyphosate	Total: Translocated	Especially against broad-leaved weeds.

Table 11.1 cont.

Active Ingredient	Mode of Action	Uses
Propham (IPC)	Selective	As in chlopropham above.
MCPA	Selective: Translocated	Broad-leaved weeds, especially on driveways and paths. Often mixed with fertiliser for use on lawns.
Mecoprop	Selective: Translocated	Good for controlling clovers on lawns.
Mercurous chloride (Calomel)	Selective	Moss killer, good for lawns.
Propachlor	Contact	Weeds in vegetable plots and shrub beds.
Salt (sodium chloride)	Total: Contact	Not good for soil structure, so best used for paths.
Simazine	Total: Contact	Amongst shrubs and on paths, etc.
Sodium chlorate	Total: Contact	Use non-flammable (non-igniting) formulation.
Sulphate of ammonia	Selective: Contact	Broad-leaved weeds in lawns.
Sulphate of iron (ferrous sulphate)	Contact: Selective	Lawn weeds and moss and fungi in lawns.

Note: Remember there are many herbicides on the market – look out for the active ingredients.

and even kill conifers. As with any garden chemical there is a certain amount of jargon which is best understood for most effective use.

Just like pesticides, weedkillers are often labelled as having a contact or systemic action. As the name suggests, contact herbicides, such as ammonium sulphomate, kill any plant on contact with the foliage. Systemic or translocated weedkillers, such as aminotriazole, are taken into the plant, moved around it and so kill the whole of the weed from the tip of the shoot to the tip of the root. Hormone weedkillers, like 2,4-D which is based on the auxins found naturally in plants, are mostly of the translocated type.

Apart from contact and systemic weedkillers there are very useful residual ones, like simazine, too. These form a coating on soil particles for several weeks or months, depending on the type used, and kill any plants they come into contact with during this time.

Whereas most weedkillers are total in their action, they kill any plant, a whole range of selective products have been developed which kill some plants but not others. There are some, like the hormone 2,4-D, which kill broad-leaved weeds and others, like Dalapon, which seek out and destroy grasses.

If you only have access to non-selective herbicides they can be used before a crop germinates or is planted in order that only the weeds are killed. Even when the prized plants are nearby careful spraying around them with total weedkillers can result in weed elimination but no harmful effects to other specimens.

Just as pesticides can be applied in a variety of ways so can weedkillers. There are granules to disperse, gels to paint on, liquids to be diluted and powders to be suspended and then sprayed on. Granules and liquids are best used in vegetable plots, on lawns (often combined with fertiliser), in shrub beds and on any uncultivated areas like paths and driveways. Isolated and especially deep-rooted weeds are best dealt with by painting on gels or using an aerosol or 'eradicator'. The latter is a recent development which usually consists of a long stick with a weedkiller-impregnated end which is touched on offending weeds.

Whatever method is used 'drift' must be avoided, that is the user must make sure that no herbicide wanders on to the wrong ground or disaster may well strike. Whatever happens the general rules for applying garden chemicals (see Table 10.3) must apply. A true story serves to emphasise this point.

Once a parks worker spent a day spraying weedkiller on paths and roadways. That night he safely returned home, ate his evening meal and watched television. As he relaxed and viewed an exciting programme he chewed his unwashed fingernails. Minutes later he was in spasms of pain and before the next day he died. It is true that most herbicides have very low toxicity but it is always better to 'play it safe'.

Herbicides represent just one step in the continual

march of progress that gardening has made since the first gardens were established 3,400 years ago in Egypt. The future is a very exciting place and so it is with a view to the future that we will conclude this scientific exploration of the garden.

12 The Shape of Things to Come?

SHORT-TERM PROSPECTS

The future comes a step nearer each day. It is an exciting prospect which is best viewed in terms of short-term predictions, up to the next 10 years, say, and long-term predictions, which will take us into the dawn of the twenty-first century.

During the next ten years there will certainly be great strides made in both plants and garden products. Because of the rising human population gardens will get even smaller. In order to help cater for this more indoor and outdoor plants will be on offer. Using grafting techniques several cultivars of as yet ungrafted species might be grown on single rootstocks, like the fruit trees of today, and many 'new' annuals and biennials will appear on the market too.

An increasing variety of flowers will also be on the market. New flower colours, perfumes, shapes, sizes and numbers of petals will appear in a wide range of plants. Perhaps people will introduce a red *Delphinium*, black rose and lavender-coloured daffodil.

Amateur gardeners will be able to breed their own plants more easily and multicropping specimens will appear that have leaves, stems, roots and fruits all of which can be cropped (Figure 12.1). Genetic manipulation will play a big part in producing new plants.

The new plants will have disease-resistance implanted into them. Already information, in the form of genes, has been transferred from the bacterium *Agrobacterium tumefaciens* to tobacco, tomato and potato plants. Naturally agricultural crops have most of the attention centre on them but there is a great deal of 'spin off' for amateurs. So the plants in the 'brave new world' will have new instructions which will enable them to make bigger and better seeds, grow with less light, ripen their fruit better, photosynthesise more efficiently and have the qualities of several species combined in one.

Many new hybrids could have the ability to fix

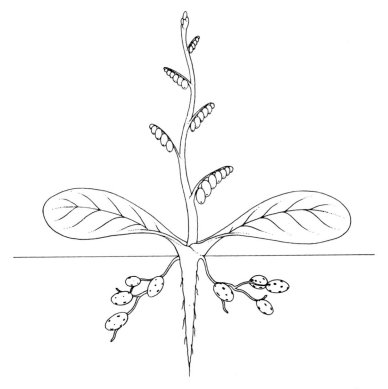

Figure 12.1 A Multicrop Plant. This plant has a tap root, stem tubers, leaves and fruit to harvest. It might also have spectacular flowers

nitrogen from the air in the form of nitrate fertiliser. They will have no need of bacteria, they will possess the instructions to do the job themselves. Even fungicides made by plants, called phytoalexins, can be built-in to every specimen so that when diseases strike the plant can defend itself.

NATURAL IMPROVEMENTS

Many present-day plants have qualities normally possessed by carnivorous species. Teasel regularly has pools of water which collect at each node. These pools capture insects before they can harm the plant and the liquid is known to have a narcotic effect. It drugs the prey and makes the drowning quicker. The leaf bases of pineapple and bromeliads all have water-filled rosettes too.

Other plants are hairy and this is thought to protect them from grazing animals of all sizes. In *Petunia* the sticky glandular hairs on the flower trumpet are known to trap and slaughter insects. Geraniums (*Pelargonium* species) have hairs on flower stalks to prevent crawling animals devouring the precious pollen and nectar meant for the airborne pollinating insects.

Tobacco and potato species have been found to possess sticky, glandular insect-killing traps and the latter has digestive fluids too. Wild tomatoes from Peru have the same adaptations as the related potato plus they produce an insecticide. The effectiveness of the carnivorous habit can be visualised when these plants are inspected at the end of a day's carnage and are found to be covered with insect bodies.

One type of wild potato, *Solanum berthanttii*, has discovered how to produce the pests' alarm signal, called pheromones, in order to scare them away. Two types of hair cover the potato leaves. One is short and easily ruptures to produce a 'super glue' capable of immobilising pests. A second, longer hair secretes a sticky fluid to halt the progress of insects. Such hairs are only a second line of defence.

Around the leaves a chemical called (E)-B farnesene provides a first line of defence. This is the main ingredient of the aphid alarm signal but other pests are actively discouraged too, including leafhoppers, mites and thrips. Already the 'scarecrow spud' and cultivated species have been hybridised so amateurs may have many more plants with carnivorous habits in the near future. If you talk to your plants, do it nicely and never turn your back on a potato because if you do, one day. . .

Sowing will change in the near future. Before long, strips of seeds all spaced at the correct distance will probably be available so that by laying a strip in a drill at the correct depth success is guaranteed. If the seeds are dressed with pesticides then pests and diseases can be avoided and if the strip is impregnated with fertiliser then plants can get off to a flying start.

One danger in the near future is that many useful garden plants will be lost from cultivation through neglect. It will be necessary to quickly identify what plants and gardens need to be maintained because they are genetically or economically, historically or aesthetically important. Then it will be essential to conserve the gardens and propagate the plants so that their future is guaranteed. Fortunately schemes are afoot to make sure that this is so. In Britain The National Council for the Conservation of Plants and Gardens was set up in 1978 to do just this and their example needs to be followed on a worldwide scale.

PRODUCT PROGRESS

Any gardener who has sprayed roses or other plants in the open will know about the problem of drift. Often other plants are accidentally sprayed not to mention the gardener's boots, and so on, so it comes as a relief to know that a revolutionary method of applying sprays is being developed for use in the near future.

It is called electrostatic spraying and works by giving the spray droplets an electrical charge as they leave the device so that they seek the nearest 'earth' which happens to be plant foliage. Virtually 100 per cent of the spray goes to where it is required and, most interesting, it coats the undersides of leaves and stems as well.

Not only does this mean that any pests and diseases that lurk unseen behind shoots will be sprayed but also systemic chemicals will reach the underside of leaves which allow absorption into the plant far better than the leaf topsides. Also the chemical will be better protected from sun and rain and therefore be effective longer.

Conservationists (all gardeners?), will be glad to hear that electrostatic spraying is very promising from the point of view of avoiding pollution. Not only is there less drift but there is less contamination of the soil, smaller quantities of spray will need to be used and spraying will need to be less frequent.

The control of pests and diseases will be made easier in the next ten years by introduction of new, improved chemicals, better spray equipment, more natural predators and use of genetic engineering to make plants use their in-built defence systems.

In the United States, the Men's Garden Clubs of America has established the Johnny Appleseed Plant Conservation Program (5560 Merle Hay Road, Des Moines, Iowa 50323) which has been a very successful venture.

Tools will be longer lasting by using more alloys and plastics but their basic design is unlikely to change. After all, the medieval spade is not very different from that used today. Any new designs for cultivating tools will still employ the lever system.

Soil will not be changed very much but potting mixtures may well be made to incorporate systemic pesticides as well as fertilisers. Plant pot material may change to one which gives all the combined advantages of clay and plastic pots.

Lawns will probably be given an annual dose of ingredients every spring which will retard the growth of grass and include a nitrogen fertiliser to make grass look greener, a selective herbicide to kill all broad-leaved weeds and a moss and fungi killer too.

Lastly, in the short-term microcomputers will enable 'armchair gardening' on cold dark nights. There will be software programs available, which will select just the right plant for any given spot in your garden given the aspect, soil type and wetness, shade and temperature range of the locality. Gardens will be planned, modified and rearranged electronically using a microcomputer before any spade touches the actual plot. Any seeds or plants needed will be ordered using television facilities and it will be possible to communicate via satellite links with gardeners on the other side of the world. Pest and disease forecasts, like weather forecasts, will also be commonplace on specialist TV links. A system of suction traps for insects plus meteorological (weather) information and radar data will all help to make this possible.

For those that do not have very much time at home but would like to maintain a greenhouse it will be possible for your instructions to tell a microcomputer to control lighting, ventilation, relative humidity and temperature within the building.

LONG-TERM PROSPECTS

Beyond the next ten years the future is hazy but within the next 20 years three trends will probably be seen: in sowing, in chemical engineering and in garden design.

Sowing seed out-of-doors is always a hazardous process. If drought conditions do not strike then plagues of pests and droves of diseases always seem to. There is no reason why, if a piece of ground is cleared of weeds, that it will not be possible to 'roll out' a garden.

Wide strips of material impregnated with chemicals and seeds could be rolled out over what is to be the vegetable plot or herbaceous border. Once watered it could be left to its own devices. A wetting agent would ensure that drought is not likely to occur, seeds would all be spaced at the correct intervals to do away with transplanting, fertilisers would nourish the developing plants, non-leaching persistent pesticides would do away with problem animals and selective herbicides would make sure that the plot stayed weed-free until the desired plants had become established.

Persistent pesticides and herbicides which are 'safe' to other animals, do not leach away with rain and are persistent for several seasons are badly needed. They would be useful both for the 'instant' gardens like those mentioned above as well as for more traditional forms of gardening.

The seventeenth century saw the rise of formal, geometrical gardens like Versailles, in France, the eighteenth century developed landscapes like Stowe in Britain, and the nineteenth century experienced a massive influx in newly discovered species from all over the earth which found their way into many public parks and private gardens. The twentieth century has seen development of many types of garden including the Surrey, Hidcote, Japanese, Scandinavian and abstract styles.

What will be the style of the twenty-first century? This, like its predecessors, will depend on the state of economic, political, philosophical and scientific thought at the time.

CONCLUSIONS

We have travelled through many of the aspects of gardening usually just taken for granted. Flowers, seeds, plant breeding, soil, compost, fertilisers, greenhouses, propagation and micropropagation, pests and diseases, cultivation techniques and the future of gardening are just some of the topics that have been covered. There are of course many other subjects omitted from a book this size. Nevertheless, I hope that you have found the scientific approach enjoyable and rewarding. Next time you walk through your garden perhaps you will see it in a new light and science will add another dimension to the multifaceted hobby called gardening. There is no end to the discoveries to be made in any garden plot, no matter how humble. To follow in the footsteps of Gilbert White can be a revelation or as William Wordsworth said

And hark! how blithe the throstle sings!
He, too, is no mean preacher:
Come forth into the light of things
Let Nature be your teacher.

Index

Abscisin 54
Accelerator, compost 73
Acer 4
Acidic soils 64
Activator, compost 73
Adiantum 16, 93
  A. capillus-veneris 18
Aerial roots 51
Aerobic composting 71-3, Figure 6.1
Aesculus × *carnea* 5
  A. hippocastanum 5
  A. pavia 5
Agricultural Chemicals Approval
  Scheme 115
Albizzia falcataria 13
Alkaline soils 64-5
Alsophila excelsa 18
Altitude 6
Anaerobic composting 71, 73-4
Angiosperms 10-14
Annual plants 24
Aphids 2, 118
Arctic willow 13
Arnold Arboretum of Harvard 9
Ash trees 2
Aspect 6
Asplenium nidus 18
Athyrium filix-femina 19
Auxins 52-3, 103
Azaleas 8
Azolla caroliniana 18

Bacillus species 119
Bacteria 61, 119
Bamboo 13
Bark 56, Figure 4.5
Base dressing 74, 117
Begon, Michael 6
Begonia 6, 39
Bellis 4
Biennials 25
Bird's nest ferns 18
Blackflies 2
Bramley's Seedling apple 101
Brassavola 5
Brassolaeliocattleya 5
Breeding your own plants 37
Bristlecone pine 15
Broad bean chromosomes 31,
  Figure 3.7
Bryophytes 20
Bulbophyllum minutissimum 14
Butterworts 89

Calcicoles 66
Calcifuges 66, 81
Calcium 81
Calluna 4
Carnations 11, 13
Carnivorous plants 88-90, 133-4
Castanea sativa 13
Cattleya 5, 109
Cedars 17
Cedrus 17
Cell manipulation 107-9, Figure 9.3
Cells 31
Chamaecyparis nootkatensis 17
Chamaecyparis pisifera 'Plumosa Aurea
  Nana' 5
Chatsworth House 98
Cheiranthus 12
Chlorophyll 45-7, 82
Chlorophytum 43, 47, 93
Chlorosis 82, 88
Choice of conifers 16-18
Chromosomes 31-2, Figure 3.7
Chrysanthemums 53-4
Citrus bigardia 8
Classification of plants 22-9
Clay Figure 5.1, 58, 124
Climate 6
Cloche 97-9
Coleus blumei 12
Colobanthus crassifolius 13
Coloration, leaf 12
Composts 66-8
Compound fertilisers 84
Conduction 97
Conifers 14-18, Figure 2.2
Convection 96, 116
Cornell mixes 67
Cornthwaite Tree 13
coxii, Juniperus recurva 4
Cross-incompatibility 30
Cross-pollinate 30
Crumb structure of soil 63
Cultivars, plant 4
Cupressocyparis × *leylandii* 17
Cupressus macrocarpa 17
Cuttings 102-4
Cymbidium 14, 109
Cypripedium reginae 11

Daffodils 11
Darwin, Charles 41-2, 52
Day-neutral plants 54
Dianthus 11

2, 4-dichlorophenoxyacetic acid (2,4-D) 53, Table 11.1, 130
Dicotyledonous plants 22, Figure 3.1
Dieffenbachia 43, 103
Digitalis 11
Digging 122-4
Dioecious plants 33
Dionaea muscipula 88
Dispersal, seed 39-40
Dixon and Joly 49
Dominant factors 35
Dormancy of seeds 40-1
Double digging 123, Figure 11.1
Double fertilisation 33
Droseraceae 88
Droughts 9
Dryopteris filix-mas 19

Earthworms 62
Electrolytic corrosion 95
Electrostatic spraying 135
Ephemerals 23
Epsom salt 82
Encarsia formosa 119
Environmental Protection Agency 115
Eucalyptus regnans 13
European chestnut 13
Evolution, theory of 41-2
Exposure 6

F_1 annuals 36
F_1 and F_2 generations 35
Families, plant 4, 26-9
Farm Yard Manure 69-70
Fatshedera 5
Fatsia japonica 5
Ferns 18-20
Fertilisers 78-85, Tables 7.1, 7.2, 7.3, 7.4
Ficus 43, 47, 93
Field poppies 37
First filial generation 35
Flocculation 63, Figure 5.3
Florigen 54
Flower structure 10-11, Figures 2.1, 3.1, 3.3, 3.4, 3.5, 3.6
    families 26-9
    formula 27
Flowering, plant ancestry 13
    time 54
Foliar feeds 85
Fossil plants 13
Foxgloves 11
Friable soils 63
Fuchsias 11
Fumigation 96
Fungi 61-2
Fungicides 111, Table 10.2, 133

Galcola foliate 14
'General Sherman' redwood 14
Genetics of pollination 30-8
Genus, plant 4
Germination 40-1

Gibberellins 53
Ginkgo biloba 16
Golden rules for using pesticides Table 10.3
Grafting 104-7, Figure 9.1, Table 9.1, Figure 9.2
Grammatophyllum speciosum 14
Gramineae 29, 33
Grape vines 7
Grasses 29, Figure 3.6
Greenhouses 91-8, Figures 8.1, 8.2, Table 8.1
Green manure 76-7
Groundsel 23, 39
Grow bags 67
Guidelines to avoid pests and diseases 117-18
Gymnosperms 14-18

Half-hardy annuals 25, 36
Hales, Stephen 48-9
Hardiness, plant 6-9, Figure 1.2
Hardy annual plant species 24
Heating your greenhouse 96-7
Hedera 4
    H. hibernica 5
    helix, Hedera 4
Herbicides 127-31, Table 11.1
History of greenhouses 97-9
Hoe 122
Hormones 3, 52-4
Humus 61, 69-77
Hydroponic troughs 98

Improvement of soils 62-3, Figure 5.3
Inheritance, Mendel's theory of 34-6, Figure 3.8
Innes, John 66-7
Inorganic fertilisers 83-4, Table 7.4
Insecticides 111, Table 10.1
Insects and pollination 11, 32-3
Internodes 51

Junipers 4, 17-18
Juniperus 4, 17-18

Kinin hormones 53

Ladybird 118-19
Lady fern 19
Laelia 5
Larix 16
Latin plant names 3-6, Table 1.1
Latitude 6
Leaching, soil 57, 64, 70, 74
Leaf, coloration 12
    structure and function 43-8, Figures 4.1, 4.2, 4.3
Leaves 11
Leyland cypress 17
Life cycle, conifers Figure 2.2
    ferns Figure 2.3
    flowering plants 23-6, Figure 3.2
    mosses Figure 2.4

Lime 81-2, Table 7.2, 87
Lime-induced chlorosis 88
Linnaeus, Carl 4
Liquid fertilisers 85
lizei × *Fatshedera* 5
Loam Figure 5.2, 60, 62
Lolium perenne 29
Long-day plants 54

Magnesium 81-2
Maidenhair fern 16, 18
Maidenhair tree 16
Male fern 19
Manure 69-70
Matteuccia struthiopteris 19
Mendel, Gregor 33-6, Figure 3.8, 53
Ministry of Agriculture, Fisheries and
   Food 115
Mixes 66-8
Monocarpic plants 26
Monocotyledonous flowering plants
   22, Figure 3.1
Monoecious plants 33
Monterey cypress 17
Mosses 20-1, Figure 2.4
Mulches 74-5
Multicrop plant 132, Figure 12.1
Mustard 76-7
Mutations 42, 108

Names, plant 3-6, Table 1.1
Narcissus 11
National Council for the Conserva-
   tion of Plants and Gardens 134
Natural History of Selborne, The 2
Natural Selection, theory of 41-2
Nepenthes 89
Nitrogen fertilisers 78-9, Tables 7.1,
   7.3, 7.4, 87, Figure 7.1
Nitrogen-fixing bacteria 79, 82
nobilis, Abies 5
Nodes 51
Nootka cypress 17

Odontoglossum grande 11
Offset 101-2
Oranges, Seville 8
Orchidaceae 4, 28, Figure 3.5
Orchids 11, 28-9, Figure 3.5, 39, 108-
   9, Figure 9.3
Organic fertilisers 83-4, Table 7.3
'Origin of Species' 42
Osmunda regalis 19
Ostrich feather fern 19
Ovary 10

Papaver rhoeas 37
Papilionaceae 4, 27, Figure 3.4, 32-3
Paxton, Joseph 98
Peat 75-6
Peat modules 67
Pelargonium 11, 133
Perennial rye grass 29
Perennials 25

Pesticides 110-18, Tables 10.1, 10.3
Pesticide Safety Precautions Scheme
   115
Petals 11
pH, soil 64-6, Figure 5.4, 76, 87,
   Figure 7.1
Philodendrons 14
Phloem Figure 4.5, 55
Phosphates 80, Tables 7.1, 7.3, 7.4,
   87, Figure 7.1
Photosynthesis 45-8, Figures 4.2, 4.3
Phragmipedium caudatum 14
Phytochrome 54
Phytoseiulus 119
Pick-a-plant Table 8.1
Pinguiculas 89-90
Pinks 11
Pinus aristata 15
Pitcher plants 89
Plant breeding 37-8
Plantlets 102
Platycerium species 19
Pollination 30, 32-3
Pollination groups 30
Potash 81, Tables 7.1, 7.3, 7.4, 87,
   Figure 7.1, 117
Precipitation 9
procera, Abies 5
Pruning 126-7
Pteridophytes 18
Pteris cretica 19
Puja raimondii 13

Radiation 97
Rainfall 9
Raw humus 69
Recessive factor 35
recurva, Juniperus 4
Redwood, tree 5
Rhizome 49
Rhododendrons 8, 93
Ribbon fern 19
Ringing 50
Ripe (hardwood) cuttings 103
Root cap 51
Roots 12, 50-2
Rootstock 104-7, Figure 9.1, Table 9.1,
   Figure 9.2
Rosaceae 4, 27, Figure 3.3
Rotation 124-6, Figure 11.2
Royal fern 19
Rubber tree 43
'Ruptured children' 2

Salix arctica 13
Salvinea molesta 13
Sand 57-8, Figure 5.1
Sarracenia 89
Seaside, gardeners 6
Second (filial) generation 35
Sedge peat 75-6
Seeds 38-40
Selborne, Hampshire 1
Semi-ripe cuttings 102

Sempervivum tectorum 6
Senecio vulgaris 23, 39
Sepals 11
Sequoia sempervirens 5
   S. giganteum 14
Seville oranges 8
Shirley poppies 37
Short-day plants 54
Silt Figure 5.1, 58
Sinapis alba 76
Softwood cuttings 102
Soil, composts and mixes 66-8
   crumb structure 63
   double digging 123, Figure 11.1
   improving 62-3, Figure 5.3
   is a living thing 60-2
   pH 64
   or peat based mixes 68
   single digging 123
   structure and texture 57-60
   test 58-60, Figure 5.2
Sowing 40-1, 134
Sphagnum peat 75-6
Species, plant 4
Staghorn fern 19
Stelis graminea 14
Stellaria decumbens 13
Stems 12, 49-51, Figure 4.4
Stem tubers 49
Stolon 49
Stomata 45, Figure 4.2
Straight fertilisers 84
Stratification 41
Styles of greenhouse Figure 8.2
'Suckers' 107

Sundews 88-9
Symbols, pesticide Figure 10.1
Synonym, plant 5
Systemic compounds 111, Tables
   10.1, 10.2, 116, 129-30, Table 11.1

Taxus 16, 17
tectorum, Sempervivum 6
Terraria 100
The Natural History of Selborne 2
Top dressing 83, 117
Trace elements 83
Tradescantia species 43
Transpiration 48-9, 92-3, 97
Tree ferns 18
Triploids 32
Tulipa 4

Varieties, plant 4
Venus fly trap 88
Viruses 119-20
Vitis species 7
vulgaris, Calluna 4

Ward, Dr Nathaniel 99-100, Figure 8.3
Waterlogging 9
Weeds 127-30
White, Gilbert 1-2
Wilks, Reverend 37
Wine from trees 56
Wood 55-6, Figure 4.5

Xylem Figure 4.5, 55-6

Yews, 16, 17